PLATO'S *REPUBLIC*
AND THE
GREEK ENLIGHTENMENT

Lut_ _ _xth Form College
F_ _ _ _ _ Hill Road, Luton

Current and forthcoming titles in the Classical World Series

Classical World Series

PLATO'S *REPUBLIC* AND THE GREEK ENLIGHTENMENT

Hugh Lawson-Tancred

Bristol Classical Press

General Editor: John H. Betts
Series Editor: Michael Gunningham

Cover illustration: Plato, from a herm of the second century AD, probably based on a lost statue by Silanion carved during Plato's lifetime, ca 365 BC; Ny Carlsberg Glyptoteck, Copenhagen.

First published in 1998 by
Bristol Classical Press
an imprint of
Gerald Duckworth & Co. Ltd
61 Frith Street
London W1V 5TA

A catalogue record for this book is available
from the British Library

ISBN 1-85399-494-4

Available in USA and Canada from:
Focus Information Group
PO Box 369
Newburyport
MA 01950

Printed in Great Britain by
Antony Rowe Ltd

Contents

List of Illustrations

The author and publishers gratefully acknowledge the following source of photographs:

British Museum, Figs. 2, 3, 4, 6, 7, 8

Acknowledgements

It would be impossible for me to thank all those who have in some way influenced this book and who would in many cases no doubt be horrified at the result. However, I would like to mention John Roberts, Jasper Griffin, Sir Anthony Kenny, and my colleagues at Birkbeck, Christopher Janaway and Anthony Price, all of whom have helped me to sharpen my thinking about Greek philosophy in general and about Plato in particular.

A more direct causal role has been played in the genesis of the work by my editor, Michael Gunningham. He has been unfailingly encouraging and supportive and, when criticism has been needed, he has achieved a rare mixture of acumen and tact. Jean Scott, editor at BCP, has also been a truly Socratic midwife in bringing the book to life.

Finally, I would like to thank the Earl of Oxford and Asquith for allowing me to complete my research in the beautiful surroundings of his library at Mells.

Hugh Lawson-Tancred

Preface

The present work is an attempt to set the major dialogues of Plato's early and middle periods in their social, intellectual and cultural context. This may seem a rather familiar, even bland, project, but it will appear a little more controversial when I add that I will be seeking to identify Plato closely with two categories of thinker that he claims frequently to deplore, the sophists and the rhetoricians, that I will argue that the historical Socrates acted merely as a starting point for the dialogues, that I will claim that the dialogues, at least of these periods, should not properly be classified as works of philosophy at all and that, in particular, I will contest the claim that Plato ever advanced anything that could plausibly be labelled the Theory of Forms.

These theses are certainly controversial, but I hope that I have been able to give some grounds for their not being considered merely provocative. In my opinion, Plato's achievement becomes enormously more impressive once it is rid of the supposition of a close connection with the historical Socrates and once it is seen not as advocating a philosophy, but as advocating philosophy. It also becomes enormously more intelligible once it is seen as a response by a writer of genius to the general opening of the Greek mind in the late fifth and early fourth centuries, an opening for which more than anyone else it is the sophists who should be given the credit.

In the course of my argument, I make certain assumptions, notably about the dating of the dialogues, which I do not have space to defend. I can only say in advance that these assumptions are not widely out of line with the consensus of opinion and that I feel I have offered at least some internal evidence, with regard to dating, for a position on an issue which will in the nature of the case probably never be satisfactorily resolved.

Chapter 1
Introduction

Plato and 'Platonism'

Plato is widely acknowledged to be one of the most important and influential thinkers that has ever lived, but it is less generally accepted that he is also one of the most misunderstood. This is the conclusion that I would like to urge in this book. Plato has been treated ever since his time as a controversial figure, the object both of reverential admiration and of visceral revulsion. Never has this been more true than in the present century, in which Plato has been denounced as an apologist for, and a partial cause of, both fascism and communism, or regarded simultaneously as an implacable defender of terminal conservatism and as a hot-headed advocate of total revolution. The minority who are more sympathetic have celebrated him as a champion of immutable ethical certainties against the threat of the relativistic abyss of the morality of convenience.

What is assumed by both the defence and the prosecution is that there is a substantial position that can reasonably be labelled 'Platonism', that Plato saw it as his life work to propagate a certain set of answers to central moral, political and cultural questions and, so far as possible, to impose these on his contemporaries and on posterity. To be sure, he may have refined his view of certain aspects of this position, and the tone of voice in which he announces it may change as his career advances. But the central core of his thinking persists, on this view, and it is this core that we find embodied in the thirty-odd dialogues which have survived. It is granted that Plato may well have engaged in extensive philosophical discussion inside the school he founded, the Academy, and that it is very likely that he wrote at least some other works which, being intended only for the internal consumption of the school, have not survived. It is conceded that these may have raised more advanced and esoteric issues arising out of his central philosophy, but it is not thought that they constitute a systematic revision, rejection or refutation of it.

The essence of the position to be ascribed to Plato could be characterised as moral realism. We can be absolutely certain of cardinal moral truths, as also we can be of propositions of mathematics, especially geometry, and this certainty in turn tells us something profound about the structure of the world in which we live and of our own minds and their capacity for knowledge. Plato builds an entire metaphysical world view on his moral intuitions.

The plausibility of this interpretation of Plato is underwritten by the stance that his work adopts towards his immediate predecessors in moral thinking. Here his vision seems to be in black and white. The most important thinkers about the right way to live before him in the Greek world are divided into two groups. The first group, the angels, contains the central figure of his mentor Socrates and his immediate associates and disciples. The second, the devils, contains at least many members of that heterogeneous collection of intellectuals and pundits whom we still know by the term *sophists*, which, indeed, they seem to have selected for themselves with pride and which bore no pejorative connotations as it now does. The differences between these two groups, and the reasons for Plato's preference, are made abundantly clear in the dialogues. Against a background of profound political and social change and the accompanying uncertainty about traditionally held value systems, Socrates attempts to find a way back to the certainty of the past but on a more secure footing which will be immune to such further disruptions in the future. The sophists by contrast, or many of them, see the moral uncertainty of the age merely as a business opportunity, to be ruthlessly exploited by peddling the meretriciously palatable doctrine that anything goes and that virtue is nothing but a matter of personal preference. The duty of the true moral philosopher is to seek every possible means of bolstering the position of Socrates and every possible means of discrediting that of the sophists.

Philosophy and the dialogue

This interpretation of what Plato is doing can fairly be called standard. It has passed into the received account of a central episode in the history of philosophical thought. It is, however, I will argue, almost entirely misleading. It misconstrues both Plato's central philosophical project and his relationship to his predecessors, to the great detriment of our understanding of both and thus of the total effect of Plato's work. Plato was not in fact concerned to advance any substantial philosophical position at all. He should be considered the founder of philosophy, not of *a* philosophy. The enormous importance of Plato for the whole history of human thought consists in the fact that he was the first to realise the peculiar nature of the role of the philosopher, which is to be, to borrow a phrase, a thinker who can never take yes for an answer. The task of philosophy is radically 'second-order'. It does not consist in the advancing of positive answers to central questions of human interest but in reflection on the possibility and the coherence of such answers and on what is implied by the fact that we can, or cannot, give them in the first place. As can be seen from an examination of any of the philosophical masterpieces that have come down to us from Plato, and in particular, from the *Republic*, Plato seeks every means in his power to introduce this new and in a certain sense unnatural way of thinking. A large part of his greatness consists in the fact that he was aware just how strange a thing it was that he was pioneering. To try to make his contemporaries aware of the nature of philosophy, of its oddity and difficulty, he realised that they had to be jolted out of the comfort of their ordinary conceptions. They needed to be shocked into understanding.

It is this realisation that lies behind the mode of presentation to which Plato remains loyal in all his works, the dialogue. The essential task of a Platonic dialogue is not to expound a doctrine of any kind, but to drive the reader to think. It is true that this purpose becomes most apparent in the masterpieces of Plato's last phase, above all in the *Theaetetus*, but the project is the same in the early and middle period dialogues. Positions are advanced from which the reader feels obliged to dissent, but the arguments produced for them are cogent and the reader is driven to think about how they can be undone. In doing this the reader is no passive recipient of instruction but the respondent of an invitation to think positively and indeed energetically for himself. In the twentieth century this conception of the task of philosophical writing has again come to the fore, but none of the contemporary exponents of it have shown the brilliance of its originator. Anyone who has taught any Plato to newcomers to philosophy will attest to his enduring power to awake a response and a reaction.

It is a remarkable achievement that Plato was able to produce this effect so early in the history of the discipline, and the question naturally arises how he can have done so. One answer to this is merely to point to his extraordinary natural talents, to credit him with an almost superhuman capacity for putting arcane points in an attractive and provocative way. This is hardly satisfactory. No sensible critic will seek to diminish our understanding of the genius of Plato, and no proper account of the way his work came into being will fail to make allowance for it. But it is quite unreasonable, indeed idle, to suppose that it can be the whole story. Plato, like most great creative geniuses, would have been impossible without his predecessors. The question, then, that we must address is what it was about his philosophical and literary past that enabled him to embark on his extraordinary project and who those thinkers were who provided him with the most valuable ammunition. There are no doubt several candidates who can be credited with a key role in this respect. The most obvious, of course, is the personality of Socrates, and clearly any attempt to deny his influence on Plato is folly. It will, however, be a central claim of this book that Socrates should not be considered the only, or even the main, influence on the development of Plato's thought and still more of his art. For the real source of his originality we must look elsewhere, to that group of thinkers who have so often been despised as mere charlatans, the sophists who pioneered the fifth-century Enlightenment.

The argument of this book

We will, then, begin by looking in some detail at the sophists. We will try to get an assessment of the leading sophists as individuals and we will also look at the background of thought that made possible their sudden and dramatic appearance on the stage of the Greek world. This task is, I believe, one that must be carried out if we wish to have a proper understanding of what makes Plato the way he is. But it is also of very great interest in itself. If Plato had never lived and written, we would no doubt be influenced less by Ancient Greece than is the case. But the sophists and the enlightenment of the Greeks that they represent would still have been of seminal importance, starting lines of discussion that have continued right down to the present day. The debate has often been noisy, but it is not clear that we have been able to advance very far from the original starting positions. The sophists should be recognised as a major landmark in their own right.

Studying the sophists and their world is thus undeniably important: it is also undeniably difficult. There are many points of obscurity. There are only a few sophists about whose life and work we can say very much with any certainty and a very large part of what we can say is derived from the evidence of Plato which, as we shall come to see, is loaded against his mentors in a number of respects. It is inevitably, if regrettably, the case that to study the sophists is, to a large extent, to study the general intellectual climate of fifth-century Greece. Nevertheless, it will, I hope, be possible to get some feeling for the individuals as well.

After we have looked at the sophists, we will be in a position to assess more fairly the career of Socrates. It will be a contention of this book that

Socrates in many ways defined himself in contrast to the sophists. He sought to adopt their agenda but confront it in a radically different style and by radically different means. In doing this, he was no philosophical naïf, but knew exactly how to carve out his niche within the intellectual life of his times. We will look at what is known of his career and in particular at his perhaps gradual germination into being the first true moral philosopher.

When we have some understanding of the work of both the sophists and Socrates, we will be in a position to reassess that of Plato. Unfortunately, in a work of this scope it is not possible to look at the whole course of the development of his thinking and of his art. We will concentrate on those works which are most accessible and which have therefore been most influential, but which also show the operation of his approach at its most characteristic. These are the four great dialogues of the middle period, the *Phaedo*, the *Republic*, the *Symposium*, and the *Phaedrus*. Of these, the most remarkable construction is indeed the *Republic* and we will be looking at this in most detail, though we will also have to consider the account that Plato gives of his own style and approach in that fascinating and oblique dialogue the *Phaedrus*.

Plato's published work inevitably stands in a complex relationship to the institution, the Academy, which he founded. It was a considerable part of his purpose in writing the dialogues to recruit the elites of the Greek cities to join his new and not uncontentiously respectable institution. But once they were established there, they would probably have adopted a very different course, or at least style, of study from that suggested by the dialogues. It seems likely that the influence of either the thought or the personality of Socrates was pretty remote on the daily discussions of the Academy, which is one of the reasons why Aristotle, though valuable, is a limited source for information about the historical Socrates.

I hope to be able to persuade the reader of a relatively unfashionable conception of how Plato fits into the Greek political and philosophical legacy. On the received conception, he is sharply at odds with the general outlook of most of his predecessors in practical philosophy. I hope that the account I give will explain more satisfactorily how he contributed to the evolution of the Enlightenment of the fifth century into the high noon of the Academy and the Lyceum and the long, sleepy afternoon of Hellenistic and eventually Roman thought.

Chapter 2
The sophists

Social and intellectual background

Mid-fifth century Greece was a society undergoing rapid and remarkable cultural and political change. More accurately, it was an amalgam, a welter, of such societies. The Greeks of the classical and the previous archaic era lived in city states (*poleis*), and these extraordinary forms of human association were of a size and character to accentuate changes and divisions between bodies of thought and interest groups within the community. It is for this reason that these states turned out to be such effective seed beds for most of the ideologies of political administration that have since elevated or depraved mankind. The city state was a crucial fulcrum for the changes which lie at the background of the subject of this book. If the nature of these changes had to be summed up, with application both to Athens and to the other less prominent states, it would be characterised, to use as part of the title of a famous book by Sir Karl Popper, as the move from a closed to an 'open society'. The pattern was very different in different cases, but all the Greek states moved from being closely controlled aristocracies, dominated in all their arrangements by the importance of family and clan connections and of the allocation of land, to being pluralistic and mercantile communities, in some cases democracies in some cases oligarchies and in many an uneasy combination of both. The conception of human association implied by these different arrangements was so diverse it is not surprising that men were led to reflect on what it is that all such arrangements must have in common, if anything, and what broader conclusions we should draw from their differences. As we shall see, the emergence of these issues was the crucial cue for the entry of the sophists onto the stage.

By the middle of the fifth century a number of important changes had begun to impinge on the Greek world. Perhaps the most spectacular of these was the changing nature of the Greeks' relationship to their surrounding cultures. This was a direct effect of the triumphant dismissal of the invasion forces sent by the Persian Empire into Greece at the start of the fifth century and the subsequent retaliation in the form of systematic

Fig. 1 The Pnyx: Throughout the fifth and most of the fourth centuries, the adult male citizens of Athens conducted huge open-air debates on all matters of domestic and foreign policy on this gentle hill, where the practical uses of rhetoric were amply demonstrated at every meeting.

invasions of Persian territory on which the Athenian Empire had been built. But trade followed the flag, and in addition to the effects of conquest and marauding there were also the subtler consequences of commercial and cultural exchange. The Greeks found more and more that they had to learn to do business with other peoples and this involved at least some sympathy and tolerance for ways of life and social institutions which had little in common with their own. A vivid illustration of this is the well-known anecdote told by Herodotus (3.38) in which the Persian Emperor invited some Greeks and Indians to describe their preferred way of disposing of the bodies of their dead. The Greeks said that they buried them, while the Indians said that they ate them. When each party heard of the practice of the other, they were both equally shocked and refused categorically even to contemplate the introduction of that practice into their own communities. The conclusion that the emperor drew from this was one which many were reaching at the same time, that law or custom is king and that there is nothing intrinsically right or wrong about any human practice. It depends entirely on the outlook of the practitioners. We are so familiar with this kind of moral relativism that it is very easy for us to forget how radical and alarming it must first have looked to many people. Inherited certainties seemed to be disappearing and there was little consensus as to how they should be replaced. There were also those who spotted what was a marked change of intellectual climate and who sought to explore its possibilities in one form or another. It is these men that we call the sophists.

The challenge to law and social institutions was matched by an equally radical threat to the traditional assumptions of Greek religion. The Greeks had ascribed a significant causal role to their gods in the operations of their world and there was strong resistance to the idea that the universe could be thought of as functioning to at least some extent through mechanisms and forces internal to it, which could be studied by human ingenuity and understood and perhaps even controlled without need to refer to divine agency. This assumption is very present in the thought of the early philosophers and scientists whom we know as the Presocratics, at least to the extent that we can tell from the paltry remains of their writings which have come down to us. The theories of such figures as Thales, Anaximenes, Anaximander and even Heraclitus and Anaxagoras seem to us quaintly perverse, but the most important and remarkable thing about their enterprise is that it was undertaken at all. They were seeking to do nothing less than give a comprehensive account of how all the phenomena and processes of the observable world were derived only from a few basic principles or causes. This is an astonishingly bold project and it is to the credit of the ancient Greeks that they, unlike any other civilisation until the recent past, were prepared to tolerate it, even if strong reservations were certainly felt by different individuals and communities at different times. The connection between the Presocratics and the sophists has been much discussed and it is hard to establish direct links between particular figures. However, it is clear that the Presocratics did much to promote the sort of climate of opinion among thinking people that made the rise of the sophists possible.

The sophistic contribution

Who, then, were these men who thus exploited the dramatic change in moral and intellectual climate that occurred around the middle of the fifth century BC? The list that we can reconstruct from our evidence is far from being complete and we have good reason to suspect that there may have been even fairly important figures of whom we have little or no knowledge. However, those about whom we do know a certain amount give us a very good impression of the general character of the group. In this connection, it is important that, although modern scholars habitually refer to the sophists in ways which might sometimes suggest that they formed a kind of movement, perhaps even with a common programme, this is very far from being the case. The sophists would have regarded each other as much as potentially dangerous rivals as potentially valuable allies, and their attitude to one another was at least as hostile, in some cases, as that of Plato. Indeed what is striking about the animosity of Plato is that it is not directed against particular individuals but against the group as a whole, from which indeed individuals seem sometimes to be more or less exempted. It has been well pointed out (by W. Guthrie, *The Sophists* p. 38) that Plato reserves his severest criticism for sophists of 'the second generation', sophists who have been trained by other sophists, while showing considerable deference to the two great pioneers Protagoras and Gorgias.

Our knowledge of the sophists is hardly enough to justify definite schemes of classification among them, but we can tentatively distinguish between the two great founding figures of sophistry, Protagoras and Gorgias, and the lesser names who should be regarded in some sense as their successors. The paradigm for any discussion of the sophists is the towering figure of Protagoras of Abdera, who seems to combine in himself all the major features shown by all the other members of the group. Protagoras is a pioneer in many ways. Indeed, he seems in effect to have thought up the idea of sophistry as a profession for himself. We may suppose that this was largely in response to the context into which he was born, as a major intellectual in a trading city hardly central to the Greek world. (Themistocles, the great Athenian statesman, is reported once to have responded to the accusation of a critic from the obscure island of Seriphos to the effect that he owed his success to being an Athenian, with the remark that neither would he have been a statesman as a Seriphian nor his critic even as an Athenian – and it has been aptly remarked (Guthrie, loc. cit. p. 41, n. 1) that if Themistocles had in fact been a Seriphian he would have become a sophist.) For most of the lifetime of Protagoras, Abdera was also more or less directly under the control of Athens, so that few citizens of Abdera had much opportunity to affect the lives either of their city or of the rest of the Greek or wider world. If, then, Protagoras was to exercise any influence on the world around him, it would have to be through acquiring a following in those Greek cities which had more clout, in particular in Athens. However, the Greek cities were jealous defenders of the right of their own citizens or some privileged group of them to carry on the business of the city themselves and were not usually hospitable to outsiders seeking to exercise an influence over their affairs. This was all the more true of Athens, which enjoyed a powerful empire, by the middle of the fifth century, across the Aegean and beyond. If, then, an Abderite was to have any influence on Athens, it would have to be through the cultivation of the Athenian elite, and this in turn was most likely to be possible if the cultivator could offer expertise which might be of use to the members of the elite.

In a sense, this function, that of providing the members of political elites with information and expertise that would be useful to them in retaining and exercising power, was the definitive activity of the sophists right from the start. All the other skills taught by the sophists – and these varied considerably from case to case – were in a sense subsidiary to this key activity. Political power was the commodity in which the sophists primarily traded. But how was political power to be delivered? The answer given by the sophists came in two parts, one very much more important than the other. The major element is sheer mastery of the ability to persuade. Throughout the Greek world, all societies – with a few conspicuous exceptions such as Sparta – were, as we have already noted, becoming much more open. Traditional conceptions of deference and acknowledged precedence were giving place to an atmosphere of debate and discussion in which whoever could put his point with the greatest force stood the best chance of getting his way. Democracy was, of course, the extreme case of this, but to a lesser degree it was also true of the more closed societies of the remaining aristocracies and the brash commercial oligarchies. It is in no way surprising that oratory, the art of persuasion, and rhetoric, the theory of oratory (to adopt a distinction which is implicit in the later literature), should both have flourished in this climate, and it was the sophists who contributed most to this flowering.

The second object of study offered by the sophists was, in effect, the rest of political science. If you wish to control or to some extent influence the flow of events in open, non-hierarchic societies, the ability to put your case persuasively is, of course, a large part of what you need, but it is not all of it. There is also scope for a certain amount of understanding of the general features of human societies and of the processes whereby political power is distributed through them. This sort of understanding can involve the study of many subjects that are, at first sight, rather remote from the daily practicalities of politics – indeed it can turn out that almost anything is potentially relevant to the task of retaining or increasing influence over one's fellow citizens. Thus out of the central sophistic project of teaching the acquisition and retention of power there arose at least in embryo a comprehensive syllabus of what would today be called the social sciences.

Protagoras of Abdera

It was Protagoras in particular who stressed the need to combine a larger and more reflective understanding of society with a straightforward mastery of oratory in order to achieve political success, and this may well reflect the circumstances of his early upbringing and subsequent career. He was born probably some time in the first decade of the fifth century and, as a young boy, he will have witnessed the progress past, and the sojourn in, Abdera (a town on the coast of Thrace) of the massive expedition sent in 480 BC by the Persian emperor Xerxes to crush Greece in revenge for the defeat of the invasion force sent ten years earlier by his father Darius against Athens and certain other cities. There is a story indeed (Philostratus, *Lives of the Sophists* 1.10.1) that the young Protagoras was taught for a time by some of the *magi*, the wise men of the East that the Persians brought with them for the expedition. This is improbable, of course, and may well have been invented to explain how someone from so relatively obscure a city could have made such an impression on Greek intellectual life, but it at least affords some corroboration of the dating of Protagoras's birth. In any case, it is probable that by the end of his third decade Protagoras had already equipped himself with the expertise and confidence needed to set up shop as an itinerant purveyor of practical political expertise. As to how he did this, we can only guess, since we know nothing for certain about his early years. It seems clear that the greatest progress in rhetoric during Protagoras's early lifetime was being made in Sicily, but we have no evidence of his having visited that island or having been receptive in some other way to its influence in his youth (he certainly visited it in later life).

A more tangible connection that we might envisage for the young Protagoras is, as already mentioned, with the Presocratics. Abdera could, on a generous estimate, be included in the ambit of Ionia, and it was there that 'natural philosophy' had most conspicuously flourished in the sixth and early fifth centuries. It seems impossible to resist the conclusion that one factor in the fertilisation of the mind of Protagoras was the intense, if baffling, debates which took place, no doubt among rather restricted circles of initiates, in the cities within relatively easy reach of Abdera. It is harder to see any precise connection between a particular doctrine of Protagoras, or any other sophist, and a particular doctrine of any Presocratic. This is scarcely surprising, given our paucity of information about both groups, but a common attitude which we can detect may be labelled scepticism. The Presocratics did not take seriously traditional theistic explanations of the operations of the gods in the phenomena of the natural world, and the sophists, conspicuously Protagoras, were similarly reluctant to accept traditional religious justifications for the predominance of the traditional aristocracies in the Greek cities. More generally, we may see the sophists as extending the project of rationalistic explanation, pioneered by the Presocratics in the physical sciences, into the area of social studies. No doubt it became clear to them, as it was to Aristotle, and still more to the scholars of today, that different canons of explanation appear to apply. In any case, a major difference in approach between the two groups relates to the fact that the Presocratics do not seem to have had any interest in using their theories to produce practical results, whereas it can fairly be said of the sophists that they were only interested in studies that were likely to be in the end conducive to the material advantage of their students.

At any rate, by the time that he had reached thirty, Protagoras had probably formed both his intellectual outlook and the technique by which he sought to instruct others. The forum for sophistic education was, in his pioneering hands, the set speech to a large audience, which was known as a display (*epideixis*), delivered either in isolation or as part of a course or programme, with a variant in the form of the handling of questions put to the speaker at random from the floor. This may seem a rather formal mode of proceeding, but it would be in line with what we know of both education and entertainment in Greece. Having perfected this format, Protagoras set off around the Greek world in search of those who would pay to benefit from it, and it seems likely that he built up in a few years an extensive and loyal clientele. It is not clear when he first came to Athens, but it is reasonable to suppose that this was always his primary target. It is very likely that by the 460s he was already well established and familiar to Athenian audiences. This was a crucial decade, since it was at this time that the democratic forces at Athens, spearheaded by Ephialtes and the young Pericles, were preparing the peaceful revolution which they were to put into effect in the five years or so after the fall of the conservative leader Cimon in 462 BC. It is very reasonable to suppose that Protagoras played more than a minor part in laying the foundation for the dramatic changes that followed.

If this is so, it would do much to explain the single most important direct contribution to public life that Protagoras made, which was in connection with the foundation of the new Athenian colony of Thurii in the strategically vital area of the heel of Italy, probably in about 445 BC. Technically, Athens was the co-founder of this city with three other states, but in fact she must have been dominant from the start. In an effort to moderate tensions among the founding settlers, Pericles, by this time long established in effectively sole control of the new democracy, no doubt thought it wise to appoint the non-Athenian and ostensibly politically neutral Protagoras as a kind of general constitutional consultant. He would have been called upon to provide an initial set of laws, though we have no knowledge of their content, and we may suppose that he felt considerable satisfaction at having at last been able to take an active part in running the affairs of a city, as he had been training others to do for so long.

In the next twenty years after the Thurii episode, Protagoras was at the height of his powers, touring Greece in considerable style and being a consistent sell-out in Athens, which probably became in effect his second home. It is precisely at this point that we should place the dramatic date of the memorable portrait of him that we have in Plato's dialogue the *Protagoras*. In the famous opening scene of the work (314e ff),

Fig. 2 Bust of Pericles: This great statesman was able to dominate the political scene at Athens for almost thirty years. He was helped by extraordinary abilities and the successful expansion of Athens's empire, but he also owed a great deal to the advice of Protagoras and other intellectuals.

Protagoras is presented as a kind of prince of sophists, holding court in the house of the millionaire Callias, amidst a galaxy of lesser talents in the sophistic heaven. When he is eventually drawn into conversation by Socrates, who is at least twenty years his junior, the atmosphere is rather like that of a particularly intense men's singles final at Wimbledon. If the account of the performance of Protagoras given by Plato is to be trusted, the large and expectant crowd will not have been disappointed.

Protagoras was a spectacularly successful performer, and it is very likely that his political advice played a considerable part in the shaping of policy at Athens and elsewhere in the middle years of the fifth century. His claims to have made an original intellectual contribution are more open to dispute. He has often been dismissed as an opportunist and charlatan, though it is notable that Plato seems, in the various dialogues in which he appears, almost to be striving to avoid giving that impression. His most important contribution, as Plato clearly saw, was to reconcile a position of extreme moral relativism with his own claim to be a purveyor of expertise about values. Moral relativism is the doctrine that moral truths hold only relative to a subject and not absolutely and it would seem to entail the corollary that no one can be an expert on what is right for anybody else. Plato forces this point against Protagoras in the major late dialogue the *Theaetetus* (177c ff) and has Socrates give on Protagoras's behalf an ingenious attempt to avoid the apparent self-contradiction by insisting that the function of moral expertise is to make the subject in each case more clearly understand and thus more coherently believe the moral views that he already holds. If this is indeed the line that Protagoras adopted, he deserves credit for it in its own right and should also be acknowledged as a direct influence on the project, ascribed to Socrates in the same dialogue, of bringing to birth the latent insights of others. We should certainly not be too hasty in dismissing Protagoras as a merely superficial thinker.

Protagoras sometimes claimed the teaching of civic and political expertise, what the Greeks knew as *arete*, as his special province. As discussed, other subjects had a part to play, but it was essentially subsidiary to the central enterprise of achieving prominence and success in the *polis*. Like all the sophists, however, he recognised that all topics were of secondary importance to the subject of rhetoric. Rhetoric, for the sophists and the Greeks in general, meant that part of the art of fine speaking, oratory, which could be plausibly ascribed not to innate gifts or to fortuitous inspiration but to the concentrated application of theory and method. For Protagoras and the other sophists this was always an important part of the curriculum, but for Gorgias of Leontini it was the whole of the art of the sophist. He is conspicuous for developing what we might call an entire world-view based on the perspective of rhetoric. As such he can be claimed to have had a greater influence on the subsequent development of ancient culture than almost any other single individual.

Gorgias of Leontini

Gorgias was born in the entrepot town of Leontini in north-eastern Sicily around 490 BC and he seems to have spent most of his life on that island, not coming to Athens, for instance, until his visit there on public business in 427 BC. This is in sharp contrast to the career of Protagoras, who left Abdera early and seems to have paid it scant attention in his later life. The contrast can be explained by the fact that Sicily, far from being a backwater like the northern coast of the Aegean, was even by the middle of the fifth century already at least as prosperous and confident as the

Fig. 3 Bust of Demosthenes. Rhetorical technique developed enormously during Plato's lifetime, and there would have been a very evident difference between the relatively straightforward eloquence of Pericles, whose death almost exactly coincides with the birth of Plato, and the extraordinary complexity of the oratory of Demosthenes, whose first great speeches are almost exactly contemporary with Plato's death.

peninsula of old Greece. Indeed it is very natural to compare the relationship between the two areas to that between the United States and Europe in the nineteenth and twentieth centuries. In addition to the general importance and wealth of Sicily, there was also the fact that it was in many ways the nursery of rhetoric to a greater extent than old Greece. Certainly the two earliest practitioners of the art, Corax and Tisias, came from that island, and these early rhetoricians probably had an important formative influence on the young Gorgias. Another major Sicilian intellectual with whom he had contact was Empedocles of Acragas. The influence of this wide-ranging thinker seems to have been relatively transient, and, so far as we can tell, Gorgias devoted his youth and middle years to building up an impressive reputation for himself as a master of all aspects of persuasive speaking.

It seems likely that celebrity came to Gorgias relatively late in his career. He may well have matured his conception of persuasion and of the nature of truth itself in the rather turbulent backwater of eastern Sicily and then launched it with considerable success in the larger market of Athens and her cultural sphere of influence. Gorgias seems to have favoured the same sort of range of performance as Protagoras, in which he would either deliver a model oration to a huge audience or take questions from that audience at random on some selected subject. It is clear that his brilliance in both these kinds of display earned him a sort of superstar status. His career was oriented more towards performance than towards instruction. We do know of some writings, but these seem to have been either highly technical manuals on various rhetorical devices and their uses (the practice of writing such manuals later became extremely widespread and we even have one that has survived from Aristotle himself, although, characteristically, it involves rather more philosophical reflection than seems to have been the norm), or simply model speeches which no doubt made extensive application of such devices. These writings were often playful and ironic in character, as with his send-up of the solemn poem of the Eleatic philosopher Parmenides. Parmenides's poem had argued that only one thing can exist. Gorgias's parody, entitled *On what is not* (see Guthrie loc. cit. pp. 270-1), argued that nothing existed, that it could not affect us if it did and that we could have no certain knowledge of any kind about it. It is an indictment of the excessive sobriety of the writers who recorded the lives and opinions of the philosophers that this promising work has not survived even in fragmentary form. It is very possible that Plato owes much of his sophisticated irony to the influence of Gorgias.

Gorgias proclaimed that, unlike Protagoras, he was not interested in teaching *arete*, so that the two great 'first generation' pioneers of sophistry both share important characteristics and can be contrasted. They both could be classed as pragmatists in that they hold that notions of absolute moral or political value and even of truth and reality itself are secondary to the practical business of persuasion as conducted in the often excitable world of the Greek city state, but they differ sharply with regard to the scope of the sophist's competence to comment on issues that go beyond narrow technical questions. Protagoras seems to have conceived of himself as a kind of sage, offering a general view of life which held out the promise of political and personal success to his pupils and customers. Gorgias, on the other hand, was more concerned to polish to perfection the specific secrets of the art of persuasion, professing indifference to the use that was made of them by his acolytes.

Prodicus of Ceos

It seems fair to conclude that it was Protagoras who had the greatest influence on the general development of sophistry as such, though Gorgias should probably be credited with a wider effect on Greek culture in general and on the art of Plato in particular. None of the other sophists are as sharply defined as these two. Perhaps the most salient of the others is Prodicus of Ceos (an island off the coast of Attica). His operations, so far as we can tell, seem to have been similar to those of Protagoras. Also born in a relatively minor city, he used his skills of display oratory (of which we have some trace in the fragments [Xenophon, *Memorabilia* 2.1.21-34] of his moral fable on the choice made by Heracles between virtue and vice) to acquire a following throughout much of the Greek world and particularly at Athens. He certainly aspired to teach *arete*, but he seems to have been even more of a polymath than Protagoras, specialising in linguistic studies and in the drawing of fine distinctions between near-synonyms, perhaps rather in the style once made popular by the Oxford philosopher John Austin (1911-60). He cuts a rather feeble figure in Plato's *Protagoras*, on which any general impression of him that we can form must perforce rest.

Hippias of Elis

Much the same can be said of Hippias of Elis. He is unusual in that he comes from a city of mainland Greece, but otherwise his career seems to have been pretty much in the Protagorean mould. His range of competences is even more impressive than the other sophists, but he may well have been rather a jack of all trades. In the two, possibly spurious, dialogues in which Plato has him in discussion with Socrates he emerges as a rather vain man and a rather shallow thinker, but there is good evidence that his display performances were the match of almost any of the sophists and he played an appropriately prominent part in the life of his city state. If we are right to put his birth around the time of that of Socrates, then it seems that he, like Prodicus, studied the secret of Protagoras's success and adapted it to his own conditions.

The influence of the sophists

These men thus became the cutting edge of the Greek Enlightenment, the *Encyclopédistes* of their day. They had the wit and general chutzpah to seize the opportunity offered by sophistry to escape from the narrow confines of their minor cities (often little more than over-grown villages) and establish themselves as figures on the Greek stage as a whole. They were the real champions of Panhellenism, the emerging awareness of Greece as a unified cultural force. They should not, however, be exclusively credited with responsibility for creating the climate of opinion in which they flourished; it was propagated and promoted through many less conspicuous channels which we have little hope today of reconstructing. The list of other known or probable sophists runs perhaps to some fifteen or twenty names, and there must have been many others who could broadly be included in this category but of whom all trace has been lost. It is also important to remember that there were hundreds, perhaps thousands, of students of the sophists whose contribution to public and artistic life will have acted as an amplifier for the works of the sophists themselves. The figure of Pheidippides in Aristophanes's anti-sophistic comedy the *Clouds* is a satirical study of a young man caught up in the intoxication of the new arts of argument and persuasion, and we can see his originals in the students or would-be students of the sophists who appear in the dialogues of Plato. There are few major or minor writers of the period on whom the influence of the sophists is not to some extent perceptible, and it is likely that the institution of tragedy at Athens came particularly under its spell. One obvious contrast between the plays of Sophocles and Euripides, who though of the same generation has a distinctly more *avant-garde* outlook, is the much greater role of sophistic devices and topics in the works of the later dramatist. It would be fair to say that by the last decade of the fifth century, the period in which the maturing Plato is sitting so sedulously at the feet of Socrates, it was not possible to attend any large gathering in Athens, whether political or cultural, without being exposed in some degree to the arts of the sophists. We should always bear this in mind when we consider the development of Plato's own writings.

Chapter 3
Socrates

As we have seen, the influence of the sophists on Greek, and especially Athenian, intellectual life was pervasive, and certainly it is not possible to offer a credible account of the objectives of either Socrates or Plato, the two greatest Athenian intellectuals of the period, without attempting to assess how they stood in relation to the sophists. The bulk of this book is devoted to showing that Plato followed closely in the footsteps of the most important sophists and especially of Gorgias and that his entire conception of the art of philosophical writing was essentially sophistic. Before, however, we turn to this, we should look at the career of Socrates, whom we will find reason to suppose also to have been deeply, if more ambiguously, affected by the sophistic project.

Two portraits

If our problem in trying to interpret the work of the sophists is that we are faced with a shortage of reliable information, the problem with Socrates is rather the reverse. We have two reasonably full-scale portraits of Socrates, as well as a considerable amount of ancillary material of varying degrees of plausibility. The difficulty is that these portraits each portray a very different sort of person and thinker. Our most abundant source, of course, is Plato himself. Socrates appears in almost all Plato's dialogues, but it is clear that in at least the later dialogues Socrates is being used as a mouthpiece for the thoughts of Plato. The earlier dialogues have often been considered to give a more reliable account of Socrates the man, but, if so, that account is still in tension with the account provided by the other main witness, Xenophon. The safest course in these circumstances is probably to rely rather on the more prosaic testimony of Xenophon, though not ruling out the possibility that Plato does sometimes report actual historical aspects of Socrates or of the events in which he took part. Against the view that, whereas the Platonic portrait of Socrates is largely a product of the creative imagination, the Xenophontic account is a rather dull reflection of the reality, it is now fashionable to argue (see R.B. Rutherford, *The Art of Plato* p. 53) that Xenophon too has a literary project, which carries him just as far away as Plato from the historical figure, albeit in a diametrically opposed direction. Both writers are creating a *persona* tailored to their different purposes and needs. However, this revaluation of the literary art of Xenophon is likely to be transient. Anyone who had the skill to create so consistent a character would probably have had the wit to create a more inspiring one.

On this basis, it is possible to reconstruct tolerably well the life of Socrates and to show how his life's work relates to the activities of the sophists. We can also attempt to understand the motivation for his prosecution and for his own refusal to avoid it by voluntary exile, as well as gaining some insight into the nature of his relationship to Plato.

His life

Socrates was born in 469 BC, the son of a cobbler and a member of the Athenian *demos*. He is unusual among the philosophers of the classical period both in that he was not born into the upper classes and in that he was an Athenian citizen, not, like Protagoras and Gorgias, a visitor to Athens from some smaller city. Little is known about the early upbringing and education of Socrates, but we may assume that it was of the conventional literary and moralising variety. The young Socrates will have been encouraged to approve the heroic outlook of the Homeric heroes and their peers in Greek mythology and lyric poetry. By the time of his early manhood, the democracy was already firmly installed and the city was being led by Pericles. Pericles's imperial ambitions embroiled the state in many disputes and these eventually culminated in the outbreak of all-out war with Sparta which began when Socrates was 38 years old. Military service would continue in ancient Greece to beyond the age of 40 and we have no doubt that Socrates took an active part in the fighting until he was nearly 50 years old. There is good evidence that he consistently acquitted himself well in the face of physical danger.

When he was no longer of fighting age, Socrates returned to his father's occupation and lived in Athens in a small house and in modest style. He had, however, by now acquired a wide circle of friends in the social and political elite, and it was becoming more and more his practice to spend time engaged in discussions with the younger members of this class. It is likely that initially at least the topics of these discussions covered the theories which were currently being advanced by the natural philosophers about the workings of the physical universe. However, no

Fig. 4 Socrates is perhaps the ancient Greek personality whose appearance we can be most confident of knowing, thanks both to extensive literary references to his snub nose and protruding eyes and to a long tradition of portrait busts

doubt for the reasons that Plato's Socrates sets out in the *Phaedo* (97b), he soon began to concentrate on his real interest, the nature of morality. What makes decisions and actions of individuals and communities right rather than wrong? It is reasonable to accept the tradition that Socrates was the first to take these questions seriously and to imagine that we might be able to reach some answer to them, or at least greater understanding of them, through discussion. It is not surprising that Socrates should have begun to be interested in these issues at this time. Athens in the last third of the fifth century was a place of intense intellectual and moral ferment. Thucydides, the historian of the Peloponnesian War between Athens and Sparta, records the devastating effect on the traditional morality of Athens, as no doubt also of other cities, caused by the plague of 429 (2.51-3). There was a stark disconnection between the suffering caused by the plague and the moral merits, in the light of conventional wisdom, of the previous lives of the victims. This tended to undermine the bland assumption of earlier generations that by and large the gods will reward deserving human beings and punish the wicked. It is evident that the destruction of this comfortable assumption was perceived by many as deeply disturbing. The plays of the great tragedian Euripides clearly reflect the level of 'moral panic' that was set off.

It is not, therefore, surprising that Socrates should have begun at precisely this time to wonder what it is that makes an action courageous or wise or, more simply, good. What is more striking is the manner in which he tried to get clear about these issues. His procedure consisted in subjecting those who claimed to have some kind of moral expertise or knowledge to intense cross-examination. The normal upshot of such cross-examination was that the pretensions of the claimants to knowledge were exposed as being unfounded. This procedure, which came to be known by the two names of *elenkhos* and *dialektike*, the former suggesting an official investigation, as into, say, an allegedly malfaisant official, the latter an art or technique of discussion, can immediately be recognised as deeply sophistic in inspiration. The technique of Socrates would have been unthinkable without the previous two generations of sophistic teaching and practice.

Socrates and the sophists

On a sufficiently broad classification, Socrates must be considered a sophist, using the techniques of structured debate to instil *arete* in those who engaged in conversation with him. He supposedly differed, however, from the run of second generation sophists in three respects, upon our perception of the importance of which our assessment of the significance of Socrates must ultimately rest. First, he took no fees, evidence, for the Platonic tradition, of his noble lack of interest in all but the outcome of the debate. Against this it can be remarked that he was fêted and even supported by his rich friends and that his tastes were modest – in a world innocent of investment trusts and inflationary hedges and with relatively few outlets to lure disposable income he may well have felt no need to accumulate capital, whose necessarily physical and vulnerable form must have entailed considerable and cumbersome precautions. He was disinclined to travel and there were few books to buy, so why bother to collect a fee? Secondly, his conception of *arete* was, broadly speaking, co-operative rather than competitive. The need to avoid doing harm was for him paramount over the imperative of success. This distinction, much iterated by Plato (who may well have been the first person clearly to feel its force), is largely irrelevant to the conditions of Socrates's lifetime. Practical morality in antiquity was conditioned by the pyramidical structure of ancient society. Ambitious politicians in seeking to advance their own cause were usually seeking to promote that of their *clientela*, their political supporters and dependants. They were acting both for themselves and for their groups, and their personal success would depend to a considerable extent on their fair and 'just' treatment of their followers. The distinction between competitive and co-operative motivation belongs among the lucubrations of the ivory tower not in the *va-et-vient* of the real world which ultimately paid the sophists' fees.

The third difference between the Socratic *elenkhos* and the teaching of the sophists is suggested by Plato to be that the *elenkhos* reached inconclusive and puzzled states from which further progress and enlightenment could eventually be achieved, whereas the sophists set a straight course for comfortably dogmatic and mind-closing slogans. This too has the look of a Platonic exaggeration. Xenophon's Socrates is a good deal less *aporetic* (inconclusive) than Plato's and there is reason to doubt that even the minor sophists were anything like as dogmatic as Plato tends to suggest. The sophists will have understood that in the rapidly changing conditions of the late fifth century flexibility was a vital intellectual and political asset; they will have both practised it themselves and encouraged it in their pupils.

The real difference between Socrates and the sophists is that Socrates was a founding member of the 'awkward squad'. In all reasonably open societies there are always those who are disposed to define themselves as operating 'against the current' and who take a sometimes mischievous, sometimes more malicious pleasure in debunking the current orthodoxies.

Such habits are useful but can, of course, be dangerous, and Socrates seems to have indulged in them with more than normal abandon, taking on the repositories of the received political, military, legal, moral, artistic and religious wisdom with a candour the more menacing for its not being based on cynicism. This, inevitably, made Socrates acutely resented in certain circles, and it is clear that it was at least a contributory factor in the unpopularity which made it possible for him to be sentenced to death. However, there were others who found this process fascinating and a group of young aristocrats emerged as Socrates's more or less permanent entourage. From about 410, this group certainly included Plato on a regular basis.

Another distinctive feature of the approach of Socrates to moral questions was his belief in the possibility of achieving a definition of a moral term and his conviction that, unless such a definition is achieved, we do not really have an understanding of the issue with which the term is connected. While both these assumptions are controversial in the twentieth century, they play a large part in shaping not just the thought of Socrates but also that of Plato and Aristotle. It is highly likely that this interest in definitions was also a direct product of exposure to sophistry. We know that some sophists, notably Prodicus, were fascinated by questions about the precise use of terms, and Socrates was probably doing little more than targeting and concentrating their procedures. It is undeniable, therefore, that the two features which we can with certainty ascribe to Socrates's 'method', systematic questioning and the search for definitions, are both through and through the mark of an amateur sophist.

As the Peloponnesian War continued, it became grimmer, like most wars, and the tone of Socrates's discussions no doubt became rather more tense. In the 420s, it had been possible for the comic playwright Aristophanes to satirise Socrates in his play the *Clouds* while still remaining on excellent social terms with him, as is suggested by Plato's dialogue the *Symposium*. As the war continued, however, Socrates's role as a gadfly to the city made him more and more odious. Eventually, the war ended in disaster for Athens. The city itself was captured and the entire empire, source of the revenue with which the great buildings had been constructed, was permanently lost. Worse still, there was an oligarchic coup with the brutal rule of a junta followed by a bloody civil war in which the democracy was restored. There is ample evidence that Socrates behaved impeccably and indeed admirably in this difficult period, but nevertheless there was a strong natural temptation for the citizens to look for a scapegoat. One thought that was prominent in the popular mind was that the gods must be angry with Athens and that this was the real reason for the disaster. The gods were angry because so many of the mysteries of nature, which were not intended to be grasped by human understanding, had been openly discussed by the philosophers. There was also a strong feeling that the city had brought many of its problems on itself through the gross lack of moral restraint of its younger generation. Here it was the sophists in particular who were held to blame. It was felt that they had encouraged the clever young to rely too much on plausible but bogus arguments to justify the unjustifiable. Most of those who would be particularly open to either of these objections no doubt left Athens during the period around the end of the war, but Socrates, whether from naïvety, a sense of loyalty or the desire for a noble death, decided to remain in the city and to face any possible consequences.

The trial of Socrates and his gradual rehabilitation

The consequence was in fact, of course, that he was summoned before a popular court on the two charges that he had introduced strange new gods into the city and that he had morally corrupted the young. The events of the trial itself and of the short period between it and the death of Socrates in prison through the compulsory drinking of hemlock have been immortalised in four dialogues of Plato. It can be assumed that at least the *Apology* is reasonably historically accurate, as the trial of Socrates was a very public event and wholesale distortion in the reporting of it could easily be exposed. There is no doubt, at any rate, that Plato himself was appalled by the outcome of the trial and that his distrust of the democracy was much increased by what he saw as a spectacular moral mistake, amounting to little less than judicial murder.

Posterity has pretty much concurred with Plato that the condemnation of Socrates was a miscarriage of justice. However, it seems clear that Socrates was at the least provocative both in the trial itself and probably in the period leading up to it. It is not impossible that he had a desire for martyrdom. In any case his death had an enormous impact on his followers, who became determined to keep alive his memory and as far as they could continue his work. We know of several such Socratics active in the first ten years after the death of the master, but apart from fragments, we have the writings of only two such apologists, Plato and Xenophon. Even so we can form some impression of the intense discussion which raged about the legacy of Socrates in the 390s. The execution of Socrates in 399 was in many ways the low point of the post-war depression, and as the decade continued the political and economic position of the city began to improve. By 380, Athens was once again a significant player on the general Greek stage, though she never fully recovered her enormous power of the fifth century. As the mood gradually lightened, revisionist accounts of Socrates began to become acceptable.

We know that in addition to the apologists for Socrates there were also those such as the minor sophist Polycrates (see R.B. Rutherford, *The Art of Plato* p. 49), who felt that the prosecution had if anything understated its case. The extraordinary success of the Platonic dialogues in fixing in the mind of posterity the image of an almost saintly philosopher disguises from us the serious prejudice that was still felt against Socrates in the years after his death. In the mind of many ordinary Athenians of all classes the name Socrates must have been synonymous with everything that was subversive and destructive to the sound government of the city. It is clear that the task of the rehabilitation of Socrates was an uphill struggle and it is also clear that it was such rehabilitation that was the primary agenda for the followers of Socrates. The time for continuing his work of the critical examination of moral claims would come later. It would in any case be a merely theoretical exercise unless it was accepted by least a significant section of the cultural and social elite. It is apparent that both Xenophon and Plato in his earlier dialogues are above all concerned to rehabilitate their hero. It is also worth pointing out that it is far from obvious how successful they were in their own time. The real enthusiasm for Socrates seems only to have got fully under way in the Hellenistic period.

It is therefore important to realise the problems facing the defenders of Socrates in the ten years after his death, the period in which Plato formed his conception of his own literary career. Their task, as they saw it, was to correct a colossal misapprehension. To do this, it was not sufficient merely to go on repeating the sober facts and hope that eventually people would listen. What was needed was artistry and skill in getting across the feel of Socrates which they intended to promote. It is apparent from reading the *Memorabilia* of Xenophon that this is what he is trying, in his own way, to do. He is seeking to emphasise a homely Socrates, who could not possibly be thought to be a threat to anybody. The problem with this from our point of view is that the result is painfully tedious. It is unlikely that anyone reads the *Memorabilia* unless they have a specialist interest in Socrates. Certainly there have been few people who have been won over to Socrates by the *Memorabilia* or the other writings of Xenophon. Xenophon was an admirable soldier and a lucid writer, within his limitations, but, for all his efforts, he is hardly able to give us a Socrates for whom we can feel passionate commitment.

With Plato, however, the position is completely different. Where Xenophon is a plodding mediocrity, Plato is a soaring literary genius. No readers of the dialogues can fail to be impressed with the economy with which Plato suggests the peculiar nobility and distinction of Socrates's bearing in life and death. Even those hostile to Plato and his philosophical outlook, including those who, like Sir Karl Popper, see him as the arch-betrayer of Socrates, readily acknowledge the skill with which he wins us over to Socrates the man. Relatively few scholars, however, have investigated how this is done. The prevailing assumption has always been that Plato was a natural literary genius moved to perform to his best by the deep love that he felt for Socrates and the indignation inspired in him by his unjust execution. None would disagree about the love and indignation, even if it might be reasonable to suspect that, as with other cases, grief has encouraged imagination, but it is hard to accept the theory that the literary achievement is a product merely of natural ability. This is surely an altogether too romantic conception. We now know that literary achievement is the result of enormously painstaking and detailed work and above all of method. It is hard to believe that Plato was not aware of this. He knew that if he was to succeed in his mission he would have to use the most powerful technique that he could possibly find. Where was he to look for this? The answer was obvious. The technique of persuasion had been perfected by the sophists and orators of the previous generation, and it was in their skills that Plato had himself been trained as a young aristocrat. Surely, whatever he may have felt about the use made of those skills by the sophists themselves and by their disciples and however critical of their abuses Socrates may have been, Plato will have accepted that he was not in a position to spurn this asset. The literary technique of the sophists and orators was indispensable to him, and he was fully aware of this from the moment that he wrote his first dialogue. What is distinctive, however, is that he was able to transfer this method across from the theatre of public debate, which was its natural home, over to the secluded discussions of the philosophers, where it merges with metaphysical speculation to become a unique and high form of art.

Chapter 4
The life of Plato

In order to understand how natural it was for Plato to harness the arts of the sophists to create his unique literary products, we need to look at his life and background. A great deal more is known about the life of Plato than about that of Socrates. This reflects both the fact that he lived in a later and more literate age and that he was born into a class about whom more detailed records were kept.

Plato was born in 427 BC into the Athenian aristocracy, and his early background will have encouraged him to be suspicious of the merits of the still relatively young democracy. When he was still only 14 years old, for instance, the news reached Athens of the disastrous defeat of the city's navy in the harbour of Syracuse (Thucydides 8.1). Conservatives and aristocrats will, with considerable justification, have seen this catastrophe as a clear indication of the incompetence of the democracy, in which major decisions were taken by the assembly of some four to five thousand people, to handle difficult issues of foreign policy and other complex political matters. As he entered his teens, therefore, Plato will have heard all around him the complaints of cousins and uncles about the foolishness of the people. On the other hand, it must be said that the two oligarchic experiments of 411 and 403 were also conspicuous failures and it seems that Plato was sufficiently candid to acknowledge them as such.

Association with Socrates

In the Athens of his time, formal education effectively ended at the start of manhood, which was deemed to be the age of 16. Thereafter the young aristocrat could be expected to do his military training and for his further education to befriend some older man from whom he could learn the ropes of success in public life and affairs. It was precisely this role that was being usurped so controversially by the sophists, and it may well have been in part to discourage the young Plato from excessive association with the sophists that he was encouraged or at least permitted by his family to spend time with Socrates. Nevertheless, it is highly likely that

Fig. 5 Bust of Plato: The ancient portrait tradition of Plato is rather more idealised than that of Socrates, often tending, like portraits of Aristotle, to give a generalised image of 'the thinker'.

Plato received fairly extensive training in rhetorical techniques and other aspects of sophistry. The association with Socrates probably lasted from about 412 to his death in 399 and took the form of the attendance by Plato along with several others of his age and class at discussions which Socrates would hold with anyone who seemed, or claimed, to be able to throw light on the baffling ethical issues of the day. It is probable that Plato himself did not make a large contribution to such discussions or engage in extensive private conversation with Socrates. This, however, did not diminish his admiration for Socrates, but if anything increased it further. This would not be the only case of a pupil-teacher relationship which has benefitted from the absence of excessively close supervision.

There can be no doubt that Plato was horrified by the trial and execution of Socrates, although he must have been aware that it was hardly a bolt from the blue. The short dialogue the *Crito* represents one of Socrates's friends attempting to persuade him to leave the city between his condemnation and his execution, and it is reasonable to suppose that similar efforts had been made, many of them by Plato himself, before the trial was even imminent. It is probable that Plato, who was himself absent from Athens for much of the 10 years after the death of Socrates, will have been deeply puzzled by this insistence by his master that the rules even of a corrupt democracy must be observed. This may have stimulated his instincts to reconstruct Socrates in his mind, a process which began almost immediately after the execution and which was in fact to some extent inevitable, given the extraordinary literary talents of Plato. In any case, it must be remembered that at this time the concept of a faithful record of the past was still very young. The historian Thucydides, in a justly famous passage, propounds the ideal of seeking to establish the absolute truth, discarding the various spins of the witnesses, but it is clear that such ideas needed to be so eloquently stated precisely because they were so novel. More generally, the Greeks had the same attitude to recording the past in the classical period as Homer had earlier shown with regard to the Trojan War. Embellishment and the moral point were more important than the painstaking archaeology of events. If this was true for the large canvas of history, it was even more so for the small screen of biography, and there is little reason to think that Plato felt himself under a particularly pressing obligation to record accurately the minutiae of Socrates's life or even to give a fairly disinterested estimate of his character. The biographer Plutarch, writing when the ancient art of biography had long been fully mature, shows exactly the same preference for the creation of a moral icon over the analysis and recovery of an actual life.

In any case, it is certain that Plato, now in his late twenties, left Athens immediately after the death of Socrates and over the next ten years made several journeys throughout the Mediterranean area. We know that he visited philosophical communities in southern Italy and spent some time in Egypt. It is open to dispute how great an influence on him these experiences had, but it is obvious that he was in principle attracted both by the extraordinary antiquity and stability of Egypt and by the sort of disciplined intellectual community that was, for instance, founded and led by the Pythagorean Archytas at Tarentum in southern Italy. He also had his first contacts with the court of the tyrant Dionysius I at Syracuse in eastern Sicily, the unsatisfactory evolution of his relationship with which was to overshadow his later years. At some time during his travels, he formed the idea of establishing his own school which would continue and extend the work of Socrates. It should always be remembered that the ultimate purpose of such a school was not merely to produce interesting academic research but to exercise power in the Greek cities. The intention was certainly not just to explain the world, but also to change it. Plato realised right from the start that for this to be possible the case had to be made, in the teeth of considerable scepticism, both for philosophy and for Socrates the man.

The literary project

It is widely accepted that Plato's first step towards achieving this objective was to write up a version of Socrates's defence speech at his trial. This version has come down to us and is known as the *Apology*, and it is rightly regarded as one of the pinnacles of ancient eloquence. It was by no means a unique idea. On the contrary, we know that several of the followers of Socrates produced similar works, and one other *Apology*, that of Xenophon, has also survived. We also know that various die-hard opponents of Socrates produced replies to such works. In the case of Plato, although we cannot be certain, it is reasonable to suppose that he wrote the *Apology* relatively soon after the death of Socrates, perhaps even when he was at the neighbouring city of Megara, where he and other Socratics seem to have retired immediately after the disaster, and that there was a fairly large gap between this work and his next production. The work, which we will look at in detail in the next chapter, already clearly shows the strategy of using sophistic and rhetorical technique to defend Socrates.

It may well be that Plato only returned to writing after he was again permanently based in Athens some time around the year 390. Whether or not this is right, he certainly began by composing relatively straight-forward accounts of actual conversations conducted by Socrates with prominent figures in Athens. The early dialogues show considerable mastery, but they are stylistically and formally unadventurous by comparison with the dialogues of the 'middle period', which culminates in the mid-470s. It is notoriously difficult to agree the chronological order of Plato's nearly thirty dialogues, but the broad outlines are clear. After the *Apology*, there are some eight so-called Socratic dialogues, whose most striking characteristic is their tendency to have an inconclusive ending. It is these dialogues which have traditionally been thought to throw the greatest light on the real character and methods of the historical Socrates. At the end of this period there follow three major dialogues, the *Gorgias*, the *Euthydemus* and the *Meno* which directly pave the way for the four great dialogues of what is known as Plato's middle period, after which his thought and his literary technique begin to go through important and substantial changes.

It is customary to divide the work of Plato into three periods, but in a sense it is more accurate to see his life divided into two halves, the first leading up to the foundation and secure establishment of his school, the Academy, and the second consisting of his management of that school and the further development of his own thought. In the first half of his life, on this scenario, his central project was to harness the techniques of the sophists to promote and vindicate the life of Socrates and with it the very concept of philosophy. The establishment of the Academy and the commencement of the large-scale recruitment of its members from among the aristocracies of the Greek cities constituted the rehabilitation that Plato had been striving for, and he now felt able to develop his thinking in new directions. It is worth pointing out that what evidence we have for the internal life of the Academy in the twenty to thirty years in which Plato was its settled master suggests that the school was not at all run along the strictly disciplinarian lines of the training of the philosopher guardians in the *Republic*. It seems clear that Plato was perfectly willing to engage in discussions with members of the school and that there were sharp and productive disputes and differences of opinion between its members. It is very likely that a prominent part was played in such disputes by the young Aristotle, who had an extensive apprenticeship of twenty years as a member of the Academy.

On this picture, then, Plato's literary work divides into the development which led up to the masterpieces of the middle period, followed by a phase in which diversification became possible. The *Republic* represents the high water mark of this early phase, but it is in the dialogue the

Phaedrus that we find the theoretical thinking which underlies the art deployed. After that, a clear break is signalled by the pivotal dialogue the *Parmenides*, and Plato, now in advanced old age, begins to investigate new forms of literary expression and technique. At the same time his philosophical thinking is also deepening and changing, and this, together with his practical intervention in the complex situation developing in Syracuse, meant that in some ways there is a decline in his literary creativity.

In any case, the second half of Plato's career can be clearly distinguished from the first. This reflects both the difference of literary objective and approach discussed above and also a change in philosophical stance. The first half is traditionally regarded in doctrinal terms as being devoted to the defence of a philosophical position which is known as the Theory of Forms. It is standardly believed that Plato was committed to this theory until his middle years and that he subsequently came to have doubts about it or to reject it altogether. I will argue that Plato never held the theory, which is indeed never explicitly stated in any of the dialogues, but that it was used as a kind of palatable and digestible version of the product of philosophy beyond which the learner would eventually climb. The theory and the attendant conception of philosophical education as outlined in the *Republic* (520a-541b) show the obvious influence of the mystery cults that were gaining popularity in Plato's lifetime. Although there is nothing specifically sophistic about these cults, it is in the spirit of sophistic technique to make use of their associations to render attractive the very concept of philosophy in the way that Plato does. We will look at all this more closely when we examine the *Republic*.

In what follows, we will concentrate on the first half of Plato's literary career, whose three objectives, as already noted, were to vindicate the name of Socrates, to present the project of philosophy in a manner that could be understood by the more gifted scions of the Greek upper classes and to attract to the Academy those cadres whose task it would be to carry through the philosophical revolutions on which the moral health of the Greek cities depended (of course, these three objectives are, for Plato, really different facets of a single one). It is a nice question to what extent these objectives themselves should be described as sophistic. Certainly, the overall target remains *arete* as a key to political prosperity, but the 'metaphysical baggage' that is now bundled with this product is already of a character sharply differing from that offered by even the most prestigious of the sophists.

If there is room for dispute about the relationship between the ends of Plato and those of the sophists, however, there is much less scope for similar disagreement about the means that they both used. Platonic technique is out and out sophistry. There is no major aspect of his literary style and procedure, including the very choice of the dialogue form, that cannot be traced ultimately to the influence of the sophists. On a balanced classification, there is only one thing to distinguish him from the motley ranks of the sophists, his genius. Plato was as saturated in the technique of these sophists as was Mozart in the technique of Haydn – both cases illustrate the advances that genius can make over mere greatness. If Plato is a sophist, why is this not more generally recognised? There are two answers. First, Plato's own partial (and often circumscribed) denunciations of sophistry have too frequently been taken at face value, rather than as the excessive protests that they are. Secondly, and more interestingly, Plato has been misinterpreted as a philosopher who can write rather than as a philosophical writer. Plato's project in his writings is not to do, much less to teach, philosophy. He advances no philosophical doctrines and adopts no philosophical position. He may well have understood that philosophical doctrines and positions, in so far as they are possible at all, have a wholly different status from the doctrines and positions of other studies. Be that as it may, his purpose is to write works the result of which will be that philosophy happens. In this he has been spectacularly successful and, at the risk of pomposity, we owe it to his memory to try to examine why.

Chapter 5
The *Apology*

Rhetorical technique

For examining how Plato harnessed the techniques of the sophists to his particular objectives the obvious starting point is the *Apology*. Though some scholars have disputed an early dating, the balance of opinion favours placing the work in the period immediately following the death of Socrates. If it was written, say, in Megara within two or three years of that event, it seems plausible to suggest – though this is only a conjecture – that a similar period of time separates the *Apology* from the earliest of the dialogues proper. If some such timetable did in fact apply, the *Apology* could be looked on as a kind of germ out of which the rest of Plato's oeuvre was to evolve. If we imagine Plato as a young man with the sort of sophistic and rhetorical training without which it would scarcely have been possible for him even to contemplate a political career, as it seems that he did, but unsure about how to respond to the disaster of Socrates's death, it would be a natural suggestion that he followed the example of many other Socratics and produced an enhanced version of the defence speeches themselves. Quite possibly it was only in the light of an enthusiastic reception of this work, at least by fellow Socratics, that he decided to embark on the series of dialogues. All this suggests that we will find in the *Apology*, perhaps more clearly than anywhere else, evidence of the rhetorical technique on which he already relied but which he later became more adept at disguising.

The first rule of oratory is to deny oratory. No doubt art should in general seek to conceal art, but that it should do so is not indisputably its golden rule. Oratory, by contrast, is the form of discourse that dare not own its name, its effects resting precisely on the veiling of their causes. Plato understood this from the start, and the work opens with a disclaimer which, like almost everything else in the *Apology*, has the ring of conscious artistry. (Perhaps, though, we can endorse the judgement of Jowett that 'some of the topics may have been actually used by Socrates; and the recollection of his very words may have rung in the ears of his disciple'.) The spirit of this disclaimer continues to apply throughout all three speeches, so that there is no point at which Plato can be directly exposed as peddling the commonplaces of the rhetorical manuals, but that does not mean that there is not rich evidence of the sophisticated use of rhetorical technique. We will first review the content of the work and then look briefly at some of the most obvious marks of its rhetorical composition.

Fig. 6 A Ballot Ticket from the Athenian Courts. Even capital prosecutions could be brought by private individuals before a mass jury of 501 citizens. Proceedings seldom lasted more than a day, and there was no judge and no right of appeal. Juries were, however, randomly selected by a complicated system of ballot tickets such as the one illustrated.

The *Apology* consists of three speeches all purporting to have been delivered at Socrates's single-day trial. In the first speech, Socrates attempts to persuade the jury of 501 Athenians (drawn from all classes and not effectively supervised by a judge or legal expert) that he is not guilty of the two charges formally brought against him by his three prosecutors, that of introducing strange deities and that of corrupting the young. In the second speech, the philosopher, now condemned, is officially seeking to reject, but actually appearing to invite, the death penalty, and in the last and shortest speech he delivers a moving farewell to the city.

The first speech

The first speech (1a-24c) opens with its protestation of rhetorical inexperience and proceeds to set out clearly the background of unpopularity on which the actual charges depend. Socrates elegantly dismisses the wilder claims made about his pretensions to scientific originality or sophistical expertise and, exposing the root of the problem as his persistent interrogation of his fellow citizens, defends this practice by calling as his witness the god Apollo. He recalls the positive answer of the Delphic oracle to his friend Chaerephon's question whether he, Socrates, was the wisest of men and explains that he conceived it as his moral and religious duty to prove the god wrong by honestly exposing himself to the possibility of being outshone by the established luminaries of the intellectual and artistic worlds (21b). The upshot of his discussions with various categories of *savant* was, however, that he became convinced that his examinees were bereft of real understanding but, since they were not similarly bereft of the illusion of understanding, he concludes that it must be his self-knowledge that the god had in mind when so richly praising him and that his wisdom consists just in his understanding that he does not understand.

The continuing project of finding out what the god really meant has brought Socrates a large number of enemies and a small number of admiring friends – but, since the supposed friends have been seduced by their admiration for Socrates into giving the impression of according a lower authority to their own kinsmen and hereditary associates than to him, they have done as much as the former to foster the hostility of the city. At this point, we turn to the specific charges, of corrupting the young and introducing new gods. In a sparkling passage of altercation (24c-28a), Socrates humiliates his chief prosecutor Meletus in open court. Meletus is constrained to acknowledge gaps, contradictions and errors in his reasoning so elementary as to suggest an incapacity even to manage his own affairs, let alone intervene in those of the city.

When he has finished with Meletus, Socrates enters what is perhaps the most provocative part of the speech, in which he insists that even if he were to be acquitted on this occasion he has no intention of relenting or of abandoning a way of life that he sees as a kind of mission. He performs a valuable service to the city by demolishing the bogus claims of those who purport to be able to advise it. The cameo dialogue with Meletus has just given us a pithy demonstration of how this is done. Now Socrates argues for its value and suggests that his function is as crucial as that of a leading general or public benefactor. He continues the list of his services to the state, in a more conventional manner, by references to his frustration of an attempt by the Assembly to commit an unconstitutional act in the democratic period and to his refusal to participate in the abduction of an innocent man under the junta (32c). He can also point to the large number of his associates who have come to support him and bear witness to the fact that he has in no sense corrupted them. The main speech ends with a repudiation of the practice of bringing forward his family so as to excite the pity of the jury. We hardly need the evidence of Aristophanes to tell us that it was this part of the speech that many in the jury would most particularly relish.

The second and third speeches

The second speech, between the verdict and the sentence, is an ironic intervention of great artistry. Socrates, invited to suggest an appropriate penalty, ironically proposes a state pension, but eventually, after toying with banishment, elects for a modest fine, promptly raised by a factor of thirty by his friends present in court. (It is certainly possible that this episode, at any rate, reflects a circumstance of the original occasion. Socrates may well have betrayed in this speech his indifference to his own survival or even what may have seemed to Plato his desire for death.)

The final section of the work, the brief remarks delivered by Socrates after the sentence of death has been passed, is wholly sublime. Socrates favours his unworthy audience with a rumination on the nature of death whose mystical tone is comparable only, within Greek literature, to the great messenger speech at the end of Sophocles's *Oedipus at Colonus*. Here a ripe readiness for death is transfigured into oracular revelation, and the apotheosis of the philosophic mind is hymned with a perfection which Plato failed to match when, much later, he came to write the myth of Er (614b ff) at the end of the *Republic*.

Rhetoric at work

We can see how closely the work follows rhetorical practice by examining just the first speech. The disclaimer with which it opens is a standard, even mandatory, manoeuvre, since to seem to acquiesce in the idea that one is showing any rhetorical proficiency at all is self-defeating for the orator. It would have been particularly necessary for Socrates with his reputation as a powerful sophist, albeit an eccentric one. Indeed the repudiation of rhetoric in the first few paragraphs of the *Apology* closely mirrors the distancing of Socrates from sophistry that is so central to the later dialogues. After the disclaimer we have the narration, in precisely the position required by countless textbooks of oratory throughout the classical period, some of which – notably the *Art of Rhetoric* of Aristotle – have survived. After initially disarming the audience, the orator must win its sympathy, and there is no better way to do this than to tell a story. The story has two other assets that show its rhetorical stamp. The first is that its very purpose is to discharge the unpopularity or *phthonos* that has been built up against Socrates. This is a quite specific rhetorical project, duly stressed by Aristotle. It is important for the orator to be able both to generate *phthonos* against his opponent and to defuse it when it has been created against him. In this speech the generation of *phthonos* is taken to be central and so justifies the main narration. The second textbook feature of the narrative is that it invokes the authority of none less than the god Apollo. It is Apollo who has allegedly called Socrates the most *sophos* of men (the greatest of the sophists), and it is in the service of Apollo that he has incurred his unpopularity. The narration combines appeal to an unimpeachable authority with a demonstration of conventional piety.

The move to altercation with Meletus was a standard feature of Athenian trials and another major topic of rhetorical manuals. The format was interrogation, just as in the *Apology*, and adept speech writers would deploy the full barrage of sophistical tricks of dialectic. Socrates uses such resources to devastating effect (more bluntly, perhaps, than in any of the dialogues). Meletus is outwitted first by an over-generalisation (he is made to seem to be arguing that Socrates is unique in corrupting the young, whom everyone else in the city benefits) and then by a loaded definition (it is inconsistent for Meletus to allow that Socrates believes in *daimonia* [spirits] but deny that he believes in *theoi* [gods] [27b-28a]). This sort of fencing was already well established and was to remain part of the backbone of the rhetorical curriculum down to the time of Cicero and well beyond.

After the aggression of the altercation, strategically placed at the centre of the speech where Aristotle warns that attention is most likely to flag, we reached the prescribed topics for the closing section. Acquittal in an Athenian trial depended at least as much on the demonstration of the good will and benefits of the defendant to the city as on the evidence for his innocence. Plato is boldly extending rhetorical irony by having Socrates cite just the sort of sophistic display that we have just witnessed as his most valuable service to the state:

> For if you kill me, you will not easily find such another, who, to use a colourful metaphor, has been imposed by the god as though on a large and splendid horse, but one which is rather sluggish by reason of its size and needing to be stirred up by a kind of gadfly. For that is indeed how it seems to me that the god has imposed me on the city. I never cease stirring you up and advising and chiding you individually, sitting and talking with you all day. Another like me you will not easily find, gentlemen; so take my advice and spare me.   (30e-31a)

This is then buttressed by more conventional references to two events in public life in which Socrates played a part which it is at least advantageous for him to recall. Three final *topoi* (rhetorical devices) conclude the speech. First comes the display of friends. It was once again standard practice for the defendant to parade his associates as tacit character witnesses, but in the present case this has the ironic twist that the characters of the witnesses themselves are evidence of the vanity of the charges. (There is further sophistry, of course, in the fact that the friends and supporters could be claimed to be so corrupt as to be unaware of their own corruption!) Next comes the rejection of the appeal to pity. Standardly, the defendant would also bring on his weeping dependants, but it is masterly to refrain from doing so while at the same time giving a graphic description of the usual effect of such a ploy. Most arrestingly, Socrates implies an epic and heroic association for himself with his reference to a famous scene in the *Iliad* (28c). Needless to say, the rhetorical manuals that we have, starting with Aristotle, almost all stress the need to recruit the poets and myths in one's support in addition to human and divine authority.

This survey has had to be short and superficial, but it is sufficient to show that there is nothing in the work which is not the product of highly sophisticated rhetorical technique. It is sophisticated not just in that it is skilful but in that it clearly suggests the author has reflected on the devices he is using and has invented refinements or ironic counter-plays of them. This could only be done by someone with a long background in rhetorical training. Such a person, in late fifth-century Athens, is overwhelmingly more likely to have been an aristocrat, bred from the cradle for political office, than a cobbler's son with little family tradition of intervention in public life. The very structure of the *Apology* is a good internal reason for considering it the work of Plato not of Socrates.

It might, perhaps, be nice to think that in this work we have the authentic words of Socrates, and it is certainly depressing to think we may catch his accents more accurately in the corresponding work of Xenophon; however no balanced assessment, on the basis of our knowledge of the immediate and remoter circumstances of its probable composition, can fail to see it not as the culmination of Socrates's divinely inspired mission but as the first fruit of Plato's human, all too human one. The *Apology* is an unconventional oratorical masterpiece, and its originality is particularly evident in the last of the three speeches. If the technique of the first speech presages the bedrock of the future dialogues, the poetry of the last points to the metaphysical, even mystical dimension that was the other vital ingredient in Plato's art.

Chapter 6
The early dialogues

After writing the *Apology*, Plato may well have paused for a year or two to take stock of the response. During this time, around the mid-390's, he began the series of travels which probably continued for some ten years. It is interesting to contrast Plato's attitude to travel with that of Socrates, who seems hardly to have left Athens except on military service, and indeed that of Aristotle, who moved only in response to the exigencies of his turbulent career. Unlike them, Plato seems to have engaged in a period of voluntary travel, effectively tourism, at an important stage of his intellectual development. Why was this? Of course we cannot answer this question for certain, but a number of reasons might be suggested. First, Plato was a member of the Athenian upper classes and as such would probably have a tradition of travel in his family as well as the resources in terms of both money and contacts both to make journeys in such safety as was possible and to stay, in a world without hotels, in reasonable comfort. It is also notable that a kind of tourism was just beginning to become fashionable in the Greek world in the fourth century, reflecting perhaps the effect of such works as Herodotus's histories and Xenophon's vivid account of his experiences as a mercenary in the Persian empire. It is also certainly possible that Plato may have felt it prudent not to adopt too high a profile in Athens in the 390s. Not only was he associated with Socrates, but his family also had extensive connections with the discredited junta of the Thirty in 404-403. It might well have been wise to keep out of sight for a season. However, it is at least possible that another ingredient in the motivation of the travels was that Plato had still by no means resolved on his career and may have been toying with the idea of setting up as a kind of sophist. At any rate, his intervention in Syracuse is completely in the Protagorean mode of an external expert called in to give disinterested advice on the political management of a city. As pointed out earlier, the fact that he charged no fee for this service is a relatively minor detail.

Similar considerations throw light on what is thought to be the problem of the dialogues. After the *Apology*, Plato wrote nothing but dialogues, almost all of them featuring Socrates in a leading role, and this fact alone makes him unique among major writers. There has been a considerable amount of puzzlement about this selected mode of exposition, but such puzzlement is really misplaced. In the context in which he found himself, it would have been amazing if he had written anything other than dialogues. There was as yet no real tradition of the prose treatise. Pamphlets could be produced in the form of speeches (we have an example in the curious document known as the *Old Oligarch*), but they could only plausibly be ascribed to people who actually made speeches, which Socrates did not do on a regular basis. Otherwise, philosophical exposition seems to have taken the form either of poetry or of oracular pronouncements, and Plato's gifts and proclivities did not really dispose him towards either. But even if there had been other available genres, the choice of the dialogue form springs directly from Plato's very conception of the nature of philosophy and in particular the nature of philosophical writing. In a famous passage of the *Phaedrus* (275d-e), he insists that philosophy cannot be committed to writing. It consists essentially of the insights that emerge from discussion. His purpose in writing is, as we have stressed, above all to encourage the reader to engage in such discussion and thus achieve such insights. The obvious way to do this is to produce written models of discussions, which may even have some foundation in reality, and to compose them in such a way that the reader is himself drawn in and becomes, almost unwittingly, a part of the debate. The dialogue is intended to sow the seeds of philosophy, not reap the harvest.

The dialogue form

Given the conception of philosophy that both Plato and Socrates shared, then, it was unthinkable that Plato, in seeking to vindicate Socrates, should have chosen any form other than that of the dialogue. It is also important to see that in doing this he was locating himself firmly within the sophistic tradition. As already noted, Socrates's technique of *elenkhos* is closely related to sophistic practice, and we know that several sophists also composed epideictic (demonstration) dialogues, just as they did speeches. The dialogue was the second most important literary genre of sophistry (if we discount mere manuals) and it is perfectly possible that many lost works that we know as speeches also contained a considerable amount of dialogue or near dialogue.

We should not be surprised at Plato's choice of the dialogue form, but that should not prevent us from marvelling at the mastery with which he exploits it. The rest of this book will be an attempt to highlight just some aspects of that mastery and, in particular, to show that it depends crucially on the deployment of the refined rhetorical technique which we have already seen at work in the *Apology*. For reasons of space, we will have to concentrate on the great dialogues of the 370s, the *Phaedo*, the *Symposium*, the *Phaedrus* and, above all, the *Republic*, but we will also look in some detail at two major dialogues that immediately precede this group, the *Gorgias* and the *Euthydemus*. Since there is a profound

Fig. 7 Two Poets. The social, technical and climatic conditions of the ancient world lent themselves well to all kinds of collective performance and cultural activity in the open air: this is the background from which the literary form of the philosophical dialogue developed.

development between the *Apology* and the *Gorgias*, however, we can hardly omit this period entirely, and in the present chapter we will briefly review the dialogues composed during this time (ca 395-380) with a view to assessing the milestones of the evolution of Plato's style. Again for reasons of space, it will be impossible to justify the order of composition assumed, which, though not wildly unorthodox, can hardly be argued to be a matter of consensus.

The Crito

If, then, it is right to assume that Plato went back to the composition of Socratic works after the period of travelling which followed the initial experiment of the *Apology*, a good candidate to be his first dialogue proper would be the *Crito*, which is the shortest dialogue whose authenticity is not disputed. In this work, Crito visits Socrates in his prison cell shortly before the execution of sentence on him and attempts to persuade him to escape, as would have been easy for him to do and may well have been expected even by his prosecutors. Socrates, however, refuses to do so, on the grounds that his duty to the law is higher than his duty to himself. As already suggested, it is reasonable to suppose that this discussion reflects many similar ones, in some of which Plato himself may well have taken part. From the point of the view of technique, the most interesting thing about this dialogue is the speech which Socrates puts into the mouth of the 'Laws' themselves, who are personified in order that they can plead their own case (50c-54d). This is a relatively modest technical experiment, but the scale that it has in proportion to the length of the work as a whole suggests that it may itself have been one of the main reasons for composing the piece. It is, indeed, also possible that Plato's own experience in arguing with Socrates about the civic duty of the philosopher encouraged him to approach this topic in his first composition on his return to Athens and his first true dialogue. It is then remarkable how rapidly he makes progress with the art of dialogue composition and in particular with regard to the structural possibilities of the dialogue form. If the *Crito* is not the starting point of his resuming defence of Socrates, therefore, it certainly represents a kind of relapse. Of the later dialogues, some are almost as short but none is in anything like so simple as the *Crito*.

The Laches

Perhaps the next dialogue was the *Laches*, which widens out the number of participants and also introduces Socrates in a more interestingly oblique way. The two elderly and highly respectable aristocrats Lysimachus and Melesias are discussing the best way in which to bring up their sons and in particular are debating whether or not to subject them to training by an expert in a certain kind of heavily armoured fighting. The question that they are confronting is whether or not such training will be good for the young men by inspiring them to be courageous. They first seek advice from the eponymous Laches, who is a distinguished military man, but the discussion broadens out, when Socrates is brought in as a neutral expert, into a general debate on whether the virtues, and in particular courage, can be taught and, if so, what this tells us about the nature of such virtues. One of the interesting aspects of the dialogue, from the technical point of view, is that the characters of Lysimachus and Melesias are developed separately from their interaction with Socrates. It is true that the situation is in some ways rather contrived, yet the characterisation is immediately vivid and plausible. In the *Laches*, we do not find any devices which can be compared with the use of personification in the *Crito*, but there is a general assurance in the handling of the course of the conversation which suggests that Plato is rapidly adjusting to his chosen literary genre. While the *Laches* is structurally straightforward, there are twists in the discussion which point forward to complexities to come.

The Lysis *and the* Charmides

There is already a considerable advance in the aspect of complexity by the time that Plato comes to write the *Lysis* which with the *Charmides* is the most promising candidate to be the next dialogue. The ostensible subject of the *Lysis* is that of friendship, and this is treated to the sort of examination which is already familiar from the *Laches*. However, the conviction is already much greater because of the attention paid to scene-setting and the more dynamic quality of internal tensions between characters. What is most striking about the dialogue, however, is that it more clearly falls into two parts than almost any other work, with the exception of the *Phaedrus* and the *Parmenides*. The division of the *Lysis* has always puzzled commentators. Certainly it is less obviously necessary than the corresponding breaks in the later works mentioned. The strong temptation, therefore, is to suppose that the purpose of producing such a divided work is precisely as a literary exercise to explore a particular kind of effect which may be useful later on. The fact that this particular device is not repeated until the very end of the first half of Plato's career, in the two dialogues the *Phaedrus* and the *Parmenides*, which are close to each other in time and may even be successive, is not an argument against this interpretation. After all, there are many comparable examples of literary or artistic techniques being explored and laid down only for much later use by their author. In general, the *Lysis* gives the impression of being one of those dialogues in which Plato is deliberately seeking to move away from an established base and widen the scope of his art.

The same objective is also apparent in the *Charmides*. Scholars are divided as to the priority of the *Charmides* and the *Lysis*, but in terms of structure at least the *Charmides* seems to be much the more mature work. Whereas the division of the discussion in the *Lysis* is to say the least abrupt and disconcerting, the *Charmides* is impressive for the way in which it evolves from a relatively narrow topic, that of self-restraint (158e ff), into a general examination of the relationship between virtue and knowledge (172b ff), a topic which is to provide so much material for later dialogues. In the *Charmides*, the discussion concentrates on the problem of the knowledge of knowledge, and it is reasonable to suppose that here, for the first time, Plato is going beyond the scope of topics that were actually discussed, or discussed at length, by the historical Socrates. It is perhaps because of this advance in terms of the philosophical agenda of the dialogue that Plato is relatively conservative in the use of formal techniques to present his subject matter. It is, however, notable that in this dialogue too there is the same sort of elaborate scene-setting as we find in the *Lysis*, and it is striking that this feature is relatively down-played in the immediately succeeding works. The *Charmides* is one of the most philosophically satisfying of the early dialogues, but it is perhaps less convincing as a defence of Socrates than those which were to follow.

The next four dialogues

The next group of dialogues fits clearly into a pattern unified by the shared characteristic that they all show Socrates in discussion with a rival expert. In the *Hippias*, we find Socrates conversing with the sophist Hippias, who emerges as something of a fool. In the *Euthyphro*, which is also set in the immediate period before the trial of Socrates, the religious expert Euthyphro is easily exposed as being a vainglorious pretender to theological credentials for which he has no sound title. In the *Ion* the rhapsode Ion is shown as having a cheerfully cynical attitude to the effects of his art on his audience and customers. Finally, in the *Protagoras*, which is far more substantial than any of its predecessors in dramatic and philosophical weight, we find Socrates ranged against an intellectual equal, who in many respects seems to get the better of the argument. With the exception of this last work, these dialogues all show Socrates in a favourable light compared with the rather shallow outlook of his opponents. This is a new feature in Plato's work, and it is a sign that he is investigating the use of characterisation not just to enliven the austere subject matter but also to position Socrates in his cultural context, as is done most memorably in the first book of the *Republic*, a composition which would hardly have been possible without these four works and which may indeed in its original version be close to them in time.

The Hippias

The *Hippias* is in every way the simplest of these dialogues. The second-generation sophist Hippias is fresh from a recent success in a rhetorical display competition and he is fully confident of his ability to deal with the philosophical puzzles put to him by Socrates. As the argument proceeds towards its inevitably inconclusive end, Hippias becomes less and less amused, though without the downright display of bad temper or the issuing of veiled threats that we find with the losing participants in some of the later dialogues. The discussion is puzzling in many ways and it is one of the least focused of the early dialogues, so much so that many scholars have questioned its authenticity as also that of the smaller dialogue which bears the same name. There are, however, some hints of the 'Form' language of the middle dialogues which have a subtlety and even irony which it would be hard for an imitator to have copied (e.g. 289c-d).

The Euthyphro

The *Euthyphro* is a more satisfying work from both the literary and the philosophical point of view. Euthyphro himself is a more imposing figure than Hippias, though ultimately his claim to expertise is shown to be equally tenuous. In fact the *Euthyphro* is a very convincing portrait of a man who is able to pose as an expert with sufficient plausibility to deceive members of the upper classes but with no real understanding or sympathy for the subject matter which he expounds. The subject of the dialogue is holiness, which is introduced in connection with the willingness of Euthyphro to bring a prosecution against his own father on the grounds of the murder by neglect of a slave on one of his estates. This would seem in itself to be an act of impiety, given the religious significance of the father-son bond, but Euthyphro in defending his action shows the poverty of his understanding of the relationship between morality and religion. The whole dialogue amounts to a very eloquent defence of Socrates against one of the charges brought against him at his trial and no doubt endlessly suggested by malicious slander before it, that he was undermining the true religion of the state. Socrates emerges as having an understanding of the implications of religion for moral action far deeper than the superficial expertise of the charlatan Euthyphro.

The Ion

The *Ion* is also a satisfying dialogue. For all its brevity it conveys very effectively the character of Ion, besides whom Socrates stands as an effective foil. It is often thought that in attacking the performer Ion, Plato is scoring an indirect point against the poets themselves, for whom he is reserving a later and more substantial attack. Certainly, the points made against Ion have a direct bearing on the central objection made by Plato against the performing arts, that their success is wholly unrelated or even stands in inverse proportion to the degree of knowledge possessed by their practitioners on the subjects covered. This level of ignorance is entertainingly illustrated when Ion is invited to explain the elaborate

Fig. 8 A Public Performance: Public performances by singers and poets were extremely common in ancient Greece and individual performers were often able to achieve international star status among the city states and even beyond them.

instructions for winning a chariot race given by Nestor to his son Antilochus in the *Iliad*. This is taken to be a fair example of the general level of understanding possessed by poets about more weighty subjects as well. The oblique and indirect character of the attack is something new in the dialogues and indicates that the progress of Plato's artistic development is accelerating.

The Protagoras

The last of the dialogues which show Socrates primarily in conflict with established experts is the *Protagoras*, which is often haled as Plato's purely literary masterpiece. The scene-setting has grown to much greater proportions and the use of characterisation and dramatic colour is more assured than in any previous dialogue, so much so that most modern discussions of the effects of the sophists on the intellectual life of Athens inevitably tend to centre on the marvellous description of the gathering of the sophists in the House of Callias (314e-316a). There are many other strokes of genius in the literary composition of this dialogue, but the most striking is the characterisation of Protagoras. He is altogether a more serious and substantial figure than the supposed experts of the previous dialogues and it is clear that Plato does not intend us to dismiss him in the way that we can dismiss them. This dialogue, for the first time, achieves a genuine balance of debate, and the speeches put into the mouth of Protagoras are remarkable expositions of a philosophical standpoint with which Plato himself never had any sympathy. The concentration on the two central characters, which is also a feature of all these four dialogues, clearly shows that Plato is deliberately narrowing his ambitions to prepare himself eventually for a wider cast. Scholars have sometimes objected to the fact that in this dialogue Socrates is made to defend a position, that of moral hedonism, which is at odds with the position which we suppose him actually to have held and also at odds with the sort of position which is usually attributed to him in the other dialogues and indeed which is at least close to the position with which his opponent Protagoras is associated. It is not obvious what Plato's purpose is in doing this (353c ff), but it is fair to say that it represents his growing sense of freedom in the handling of the historical Socrates as a character in his dialogues.

A transitional dialogue: the Meno

Before moving on to consider the *Gorgias* and the *Euthydemus*, we must look finally at the other dialogue that belongs with this group, the *Meno*.

The *Meno* is unquestionably an important work, introducing two themes, the doctrine of knowledge by recollection, and the sketch of dialectical method, which have an important influence on the dialogues that follow. However, in terms of the art of its composition, it shows rather less attention to detail than in the immediately preceding works, as we would expect for what is in certain ways a transitional dialogue. There is no elaborate *mise-en-scène* and the dialogue begins more abruptly than any other. The character of Meno, the principal interlocutor, is slightly insipid, but that of Socrates's future prosecutor Anytus, who makes a brief intervention, is altogether more effective in its sinister combination of pomposity and menace:

> Socrates, you seem to find it rather easy to be rude about people. I would warn you, if you are prepared to listen, to take care. I don't know whether in other cities it is easier to do people harm than good, but it certainly is in this one. But I think you don't need to be told this.   (94e-95a)

The most entertaining part of the dialogue, however, is the celebrated 'thought experiment', in which Socrates extracts geometrical proofs from an untrained slave boy and so shows that he must have had this knowledge in some sense in him from birth (82b-85b). This is perhaps an ironic reference to the oratorical practice of cross-examining expert witnesses – the whole point about this witness is that he is precisely not an expert. Otherwise, the *Meno* is curiously like those later dialogues in which the philosophical development going on inside Plato's own thinking elbows out the elaborate deployment of rhetorical artistry. In terms of pure art, we should regard it as something of a pause before the major advances to come.

This survey of the early dialogues has had to be extremely brief, but any consideration of these works shows a writer with remarkable inventiveness and willingness to experiment in his attempts to achieve his desired effects of subtlety, variety, animation and drama. These dialogues were Plato's sophistic and rhetorical apprenticeship, and the long phase of evolution that they represent was indispensable for achieving the mastery of the great works that we have yet to consider.

Chapter 7
The *Gorgias* and the *Euthydemus*

In this chapter we will look at the two dialogues which may well have been the last Plato wrote before he embarked on the four masterpieces of the 'middle period'. It is, as always, impossible to be confident of any precise dating, but it would seem reasonably clear on internal grounds that these two works must lie towards the end of the period of maturation of Plato's art. They are both rhetorical masterpieces, yet they could hardly be more sharply contrasted in tone. The *Gorgias* is a profound rumination on the nature of rhetoric, ending in a spectacular show-down which sharply illustrates the dangers of its misuse, while the *Euthydemus* is a brilliant intellectual comedy, which should perhaps be classified as a brilliant *exercise en style*. For all their differences, they both clearly show how ready Plato is to embark on his four central dialogues.

The Gorgias *and rhetoric*

If the *Apology* is the work in which Plato first commits the sin of oratory, the *Gorgias* is that in which he most strenuously denies it. The denial, however, has that degree of excess which smacks of addiction, and in the *Republic* and, especially, the *Phaedrus*, the need to disclaim, in effect, the rhetorical basis of Plato's style is far less strongly felt. It is perhaps regrettable that the *Gorgias*, with its extraordinary attack on its author's own profession, should have attracted so much of the limelight from Plato's later and more balanced treatments of rhetoric, but that it has done so is evidence of the remarkable construction and sustained philosophical vigour of this work.

Even in the *Gorgias*, however, there are signs that Plato is keener to attack rhetoric in its consequences than in its essence. The character of Gorgias himself, the embodiment of rhetorical theory, is treated with deference, whereas the immature Polus is humiliated before the spectacular confrontation between Socrates and the sinister Callicles. By the time of the presumable dramatic date of the dialogue, Gorgias is an elderly and distinguished figure, who has made a contribution to, or at least had a view on, a variety of intellectual debates in addition to oratory.

We are given the impression that he has had the mantle of sophistry thrust upon him. Rather like Haydn, he is travelling abroad in later life to discover a celebrity of which he had not previously been aware.

The work opens without ceremony (the start has the same sort of businesslike impatience as the *Meno*), and after a perfunctory introduction to its participants, Socrates, his friend Chaerephon, the grandee Callicles, Gorgias himself and his acolyte Polus, we get straight down to work. The dialogue is divided into three distinct acts, whose harmoniously evolving sequence is one of its pleasures, each act being a conversation between Socrates and one of the proponents of rhetoric. In the first, and slightest, conversation, with Gorgias himself (449a-461b), Chaerephon is thrown in as a kind of skirmisher. He is told to ask Gorgias the bald enough question, who he is. Any reply from Gorgias is forestalled by the interposition of Polus whose pretentious and effect-seeking response cues a demand from Socrates for answers rather than speeches. Gorgias, unlike his pupil, is ready to reply in this kind, and a discussion ensues marked by the studied brevity of his interventions. In the course of it, Socrates harries Gorgias into accepting a definition of rhetoric as the art of persuading the ignorant by the ignorant. Whereas genuine expertise in some field all too often goes unrecognised, the meretricious sound-bites of the rhetorician earn him an esteem and prestige wholly unjustified by his real grasp of the subjects that he professes to have mastered. In particular, the rhetorician will be able to prate at length about the virtues without being in reality able to tell a genuine moral action from a sham one. Gorgias, unable to escape from this predicament, is forced to the patently *ad hoc* manoeuvre of stipulating that ethics must always be a kind of obligatory supplement to a course in rhetoric.

At this point Gorgias is permitted to retire, and Polus, horrified at the consequences of being on the receiving end of the *elenkhos*, insists on turning the tables, so that, if he is not to be permitted to pontificate, then at least he must be allowed to ask rather than to suffer the fate of having to answer the questions. In fact, although Polus is allowed to be the interviewer, he soon finds himself fed questions by the interviewee. Thus, having asked what rhetoric is and received the reply that it is a skill for producing a certain kind of pleasure, he is then charged to ask what cooking is, a commission he promptly discharges. This enables Socrates to classify both cooking and rhetoric in the same genus, so that the task of defining it now reduces to the discovery of its specific hallmark within this genus (464b-466a). This broadens into a kind of taxonomy (classification) of the arts, based on the distinctions between body and soul and between semblance and reality. Thus there are two arts in reality ministering to the body, gymnastics and medicine, and two ministering to the soul, justice and legislation (think of them as morality and political leadership). Each of these real arts has a kind of bogus shadow, with sartorial fashion apeing gymnastics, cookery medicine, rhetoric morality and sophistry the supreme art of politics. Polus protests that this excessively pejorative allocation of a role to rhetoric belies its vast power to sway the counsels of men. Surely such capacities are not to be confused with a mere knack of pandering to the over-excited cravings of the disordered mind. And he passes to a roll call of heroes of rhetorical cynicism who have harnessed its powers to the promotion of their own unbounded ambitions.

Polus is claiming that the quintessence of the utility of rhetoric is that it enables a person to do harm with impunity, and Socrates now seeks to show him that if that is the case it can only be injurious to its possessor, since doing harm in any form is a personal disaster for the doer and doing harm without punishment is worse still:

> So, for the purpose of providing a defence for one's own crimes, or those of one's parents, one's friends or one's children, or of one's country if it is in the wrong, rhetoric is of no use to us, Polus, unless one were to assign it the opposite role – that of accusing oneself and after that one's relations and anyone else of one's friends who may be in the wrong and, far from hiding, of actually bringing to light the crime, so that I may be punished and become whole again. (480b-c)

This argument foreshadows the more extensive defence of the same point in the *Republic*. In the present dialogue, the reasoning to which Socrates resorts is the most absurdly fallacious in the entire corpus. It turns on equations, of bottomless triviality, between evil-doing and 'foulness', and 'foulness' and being in an undesirable state. It is impossible that Plato intended this argument to be taken seriously as it stands, but it is less clear what his real purpose is in introducing it. The most plausible explanation is the desire to expose the vulnerability of Polus to the tricks of the sophist. Thus just as morality falls below politics, so does rhetoric, its shadow, fall below sophistry, the shadow of political knowledge. It remains only for Socrates to complete the humiliation of Polus by obtaining from him the grudging concession that to be foul without hope of redemption, i.e., to wrong without the possibility of being corrected, is to be in the worst of all possible positions and that it is in precisely this predicament that one is likely to be landed by an excessive mastery of rhetoric (480b-c).

Up to the point of the dismissal of Polus, the *Gorgias* is not unlike the *Hippias* and the dialogue that became the first book of the *Republic*. The final conversation, with Callicles (481b-522e), lifts the work into a different level by providing Socrates with a worthy interlocutor, his first since the *Protagoras*. Callicles has drunk deep where Polus has merely sipped. The latter has a somewhat detached and puerile admiration for the villains that he purports to revere, but the former is itching to enter their ranks. His ambition has led him to embrace a distinction which, he feels, with many subsequent thinkers, would have saved Polus. Polus moved too easily from the premise that evil-doing is the object of disapproval to the conclusion that it is a bad thing for the doer. In making this transition, he showed himself to be a slave to the conventional morality. In the terms of conventional morality, the conclusion to which Socrates drove Polus must be right. If it is frowned on by the majority of men, it must be wrong. This, however, only shows that conventional morality, requiring as it does the subordination of the instincts of self-assertion, is in some sense deeply unnatural. In the morality of nature, self-assertion is admirable and good and it is humility and the acceptance of insult that is foul. Rhetoric enables anyone who realises this to forward his schemes. In this respect, it is superior to philosophy, which, after a certain pubescent charm, can achieve only the befuddling of the wits and the loss of the name of action by one's natural projects. Rhetoric springs from the deepest instincts of human nature, philosophy from their retarded development.

The morality of power of Callicles has often been compared with that of Nietzsche, just as the dismissal of morality as a tool of social manipulation by Thrasymachus has often been assimilated to the dismissal of bourgeois morality as an offshoot of the distribution of property by the more vulgar followers of Marx. In fact, Callicles's position is uncluttered by the extraordinary ideological baggage of Nietzsche, just as Thrasymachus is innocent of the ponderous metaphysics of Marx. The two Greeks manifest two natural forms that a distrust for the philosopher's pretensions to moral certainty can take. It would seem that at certain periods these have received especially eloquent expression.

Socrates's way with Callicles is to show that his position rests on a hedonistic analysis of happiness and then to demonstrate the untenability of such an account. He develops various paradoxes of hedonism, and, when Callicles is at last constrained to admit that the good is necessarily distinct from the pleasant, the schema of the arts that emerged in the discussion with Polus is revived and Callicles is forced to acknowledge that rhetoric is to be found among the shadow, not the real, skills. At this point, Callicles withdraws, at least for a time, and Socrates in a rambling speech (507c-509d) recapitulates most of the points that have so far been established in the discussion. When Callicles rejoins the discussion, he stresses, rather surprisingly, that rhetoric, if not a source of power, is at least a source of security. It is important to remember that in ancient Athens members of the political class were indeed constantly exposed to the threat of litigious or political attack, the outcome of which could be their exile or even death. In practice, their only real defence was the art of the rhetorician (which custom required that they used themselves rather than, as in Rome, employing a Cicero). Socrates, however, insists that to be defended in injustice is not really to be defended at all, and he concludes by an historical excursus debunking the claims of the great statesmen of Athens, heroes of the rhetoricians, to have made contributions to the moral education of the people. This is followed by a myth which, as in the *Republic*, carries on the reward of the good man into the next life.

The *Gorgias* is Socrates's most successful integration so far of the evolution of an argument with the drama of a discussion. It covers much the same ground as the *Republic*, and the attempt to compose the longer work must have been to a great extent stimulated by the artistic success of the shorter. The denial of rhetoric is a kind of descendant, on a huge scale, of the similar denial in the *Apology*. Before embarking on the most rhetorical phase of his career, Plato felt the need once again to renew his insistence that Socrates was different from the other sophists and, by the same token, he, Plato, is different from the other orators. However, the disclaimer is already more subtle than that in the *Apology* and prepares the way for the acknowledgement of rhetoric in the *Phaedrus*. It would be perverse, to be sure, to propose the sub-title *In Praise of Rhetoric* for the *Gorgias*, as it would not be for the *Phaedrus*, but it is very clear that Plato's target is not the art itself, as embodied by Gorgias, so much as its shallow and inept interpretation, as represented by Polus, and still more its cynical and amoral exploitation, for which Callicles is so effectively exposed. Only after a strenuous condemnation of the abuse of rhetoric was it possible to argue for its legitimate role in philosophical discourse – only after the *Gorgias* was the *Phaedrus* possible.

The Euthydemus

If the *Gorgias* puts down a marker for Plato later to defend the higher art of rhetoric as he conceives it, the *Euthydemus* is Plato's comedy of manners, and it is also one of the most nearly perfect dramatic structures in Greek literature. It would be, if anything, generous to the source to suggest the influence of Aristophanes. In addition to all this, it even finds time for some philosophy.

It is, as already pointed out, one of the principal tasks of the early dialogues to imply a contrast between the sophistic and the Socratic styles of moral and philosophical discussion. Usually, however, the contrast emerges indirectly in the course of the attempt to get clear about the puzzle of the moment. In the *Euthydemus*, on the other hand, it could be said that style is everything and that the contrast of approaches takes centre stage. Moreover, the whole arrangement is handled with consummate skill which removes any danger that the proceedings might degenerate into mere formality.

The sureness of touch begins with the choice and characterisation of the participants and especially of Socrates's main opponents, the brother sophists Euthydemus and Dionysodorus. These two figures are good examples of the bandwagon variety of sophist. Having failed to make their way, Socrates implies, in military training, they are turning to the fashionable teaching of virtue as a shortcut to fame and fortune (271c ff). This a bit like giving up running an aerobics gym to become a tele-evangelist. Plato and his Socrates have some time for major intellectual figures such as Protagoras and Gorgias but only contempt for such vainglorious windbags as Prodicus and Hippias, abhorrence for such petulant thugs as Thrasymachus and Callicles and amusement at the antics of such hangers-on of the sophistic profession as Meno, Polus or, in the present dialogue, Euthydemus and Dionysodorus. These last two were colonials from Thurii in the Greek Wild West of Southern Italy, but had been hanging around Athens for some time hoping to cash in on their pretensions to provide a quick fix to becoming virtuous.

All this is fluently conveyed in the double introduction (271a-274d), in which Socrates is asked by his friend Crito to recall the conversation of the previous day with the two sophists and a crowd of on-lookers and, in doing so, provides further details of the occasion and those taking part. The main discussion is thus narrated by Socrates to Crito (though Crito does make one brief interruption). It is devoted to the question how best to persuade possible students of virtue that it is in their interests to engage in this pursuit. It becomes thus a display of rivalry in the art of protreptic, or inducement to philosophy, which is reminiscent of the rival displays of the poets in Aristophanes's *Frogs* and may indeed owe something either to that passage itself or to the genre to which it belongs. It is structured in such a way that the presentation of the sophists, which reaches bizarre extremes of perverse ingenuity, is interlaced with that of

Socrates, which bears the stamp of his authentic interest in moral conduct and in the philosophy that underpins it.

When, therefore, Euthydemus and Dionysodorus begin the task of persuading the young Athenian aristocrat Cleinias, who is taken as the guinea pig for both presentations, they do so in a way that is both strange and revealing of their whole stance (275d ff). It is at once clear that they are among those teachers who believe that the first stage of education is to produce an appropriate sense of awe in the pupil. Accordingly, they put some innocent sounding questions to Cleinias and immediately show that whatever answer he gives he will be drawn into contradiction or absurdity. This strategy, of asking questions the answers to which can only lead to logical confusion, was something of a minor art form flourishing among Greek intellectuals of the fifth and fourth centuries. It is known as eristics, which literally means the asking of vexatious questions so as to convince the hearer of his own ignorance and bafflement where he took himself to be possessed of certainty. It has very often been pointed out that this is remarkably reminiscent of the activity that Plato ascribes to Socrates, and one of the major tasks of the early dialogues is to show the difference between mere eristics and the serious examination, the so-called *elenkhos*, in which Socrates is engaged. It is the present dialogue above all that is devoted to this. The central theme is that the eristical exercises of the sophists are wholly shallow and rest on simple, indeed puerile, devices, while the *elenkhos* has the profoundly constructive task of showing that vital areas of knowledge and understanding for our moral lives are much more obscure and perplexing than we realised. From this point of view, the opening contributions of Euthydemus and Dionysodorus in this first of the three sections of their protreptic exercise are footling enough, although, for all their absurdity, they are greeted with ecstatic enthusiasm by the *claque* in the sophists' entourage.

Socrates intervenes, to relieve, as he tells us, the strain on Cleinias who is being initiated into the strange rituals of the sophists (288b). He explains the ostensible purpose behind the extraordinary and apparently vacuous wordplay, only to dismiss it as being unlikely to conduce to any real advance in understanding in the pupil. He then launches into his own exposition, which begins with his obtaining from Cleinias the concession of the relatively uncontroversial point that everybody wants success. This is a variant on the premise of many of Socrates's arguments, notably in the *Gorgias*, that, in some sense or other, everybody seeks the good. From this starting point, Socrates walks Cleinias through a number of very plausible advances. Success flows not from the mere possession, but from the possession and enjoyment, of good things and, more particularly, from the right enjoyment of such things. But it is only by virtue of our possession of wisdom that we can tell what the right enjoyment is of any advantage that we may have. So wisdom is an indispensable precondition of success and philosophy, the pursuit of wisdom, is an inescapable obligation of any rational subject. This sort of argument is much repeated in later ancient philosophy, becoming a kind of cliché. In one version, the nice twist is added that even in debating whether or not one is to engage in philosophy one is already philosophising, so that philosophy is not merely desirable but inevitable (305e ff). The key feature of its introduction in the *Euthydemus* is that the thrust of the argument is intuitively palatable, or at least serious, whatever formal fallacies may disfigure its surface. This already affords a contrast with the gratuitous and vapid complexity of Socrates's sophistic rivals.

The sophists, for their part, are wholly unadmonished by their exposure to true philosophy and at once embark on a barrage of fallacies which continues, interrupted only by Socrates's second episode (291b-297b), until the end of the dialogue. The hallmark of this pyrotechnic display of the apotheosis of the footling is that the triviality of the treatment so often and so starkly contrasts with the profundity of the material. There are, for instance, deep issues connected with the concepts of non-being and of misrepresentation, of which Plato frequently shows himself to be very well aware, but these subjects are taken by Euthydemus and Dionysodorus as the merest pretexts for yet more sophistic gymnastics.

Socrates's second interruption is motivated, like his first, by the desire to prevent overstrain in Cleinias. He resumes his argument from where it had reached, the conclusion that the universal desire for success entails the pursuit of philosophy. But what more can we say about philosophy other than the etymological remark that it is the pursuit of wisdom? It is here that the *Euthydemus* comes closest to doing some real intellectual work (305e ff). The person who turns to philosophy as a guide to life will be looking for a kind of skill, the skill of living (such is the constant assumption, now though unfruitful, of the Socratic dialogues), but on examination it turns out that this skill must be radically different from any other skill. All other skills produce some result or other, but this skill must also be able to equip us with the knowledge how to make best use of its own product, and neither Cleinias nor Socrates can think of any skill that is very like that. Crito himself is drawn into the discussion, which comes to focus on the art of monarchy or political rule, which at least has the property of being that art which in a sense governs all the others. However, it seems that even this cannot be the object of philosophy, since it does not involve any particular knowledge of the kind that would enable us always to act rightly rather than merely competently. We might comment that this second Socratic episode in the main discussion (to which any contribution by Euthydemus and Dionysodorus would be wholly inappropriate) shows that Plato's thought is beginning to outgrow the association of the moral life with the mastery of a skill that he had probably inherited from Socrates. Plato is aware that this is a momentous development, since it shows that moral insight and knowledge has a character much stranger than that of any other form of human expertise or capacity. The way forward in this debate is far from clear, but the importance of the journey is apparent.

Just as we are glimpsing the shadowy outlines of philosophical *terra firma* on the horizon, we are swept back out to the open sea of eristics by the final tidal wave of fallacies and sophisms from the dynamic duo (297b ff). There is nothing in Plato to compare with the sheer effervescence with which the relentless and wholly fatuous ingenuity of the brothers swamps all attempts to initiate some meaningful line of discussion. The whole passage is a *tour de force* of *bravura* brilliance, spangled with strokes of irony and of a sublime levity that makes it the cheese soufflé of ancient philosophy. When it comes finally to an end, Crito is in a state of profound ambivalence as to whether or not to subject his sons to philosophy, but we ourselves are unclear whether he is emptily or pregnantly unclear.

The *Euthydemus* attempts that hardest of tasks for the popular expounder of philosophy, the task of clarifying to the layman the distinction between difficult, strange and important discourse and difficult, strange and completely pointless discourse. This battle must constantly be refought, but those engaged in it would be doing well if they could enter the fray with the elegant irony and sheer satirical panache displayed by Plato in this most sympathetic of his works.

With these two dialogues, Plato's style can be said to have come fully of age. He has now shown how it is possible to integrate every aspect of rhetorical technique while holding together the consistent characterisation of his hero. He has shown mastery in handling all aspects of a conversation, from the relaxed and even lyrical to the intense and eristic, and of moving seamlessly from one phase of a discussion to another. He is now in a position to put the greater weight of metaphysical speculation on the structure that he has created and to infuse his presentation of the discussions with a greater philosophical intensity than ever before. It is not surprising that he should have chosen to do so first in the dialogue which is set on the actual occasion of Socrates's death.

Chapter 8
The *Phaedo*

It is on the *Phaedo*, more than any other dialogue, that the vindication – better, the apotheosis – of Socrates rests. The other three dialogues of what now becomes a group of four works describing his death have prepared us for the effect of the *Phaedo*. In the *Euthyphro* we see Socrates at his most ironically deferential and urbane in dealing with the self-important and shallow Euthyphro, in the *Apology* he reduces his opponents to stammering incoherence and at the same time displays a lofty hauteur towards those who are presuming to judge him and in the *Crito* he shows us that even in the isolation of his cell he has lost none of his preference for death over dishonour. But it is in the *Phaedo* that our admiration is most intensely aroused, as we see the sage unflinchingly embrace a grave whose victory he has just demolished with a swan-song of reasoning that tramples under foot the serpent of materialistic pessimism.

Setting (57a-63b)

The *Phaedo* describes the conversation that supposedly occupied the last day of Socrates's life. Socrates discusses extensively the doctrine of the immortality of the soul, confronts, assesses and roundly sees off a range of objections. To the cynical perspective of the late twentieth century it appears strange that the dialogue has so often been taken at its face value, as a semi-historical account of the actual events surrounding the death of Socrates. The integration of doctrine and demeanour, of content and character, of instruction and example, is too complete, the hero's eloquent valediction too sublime, for us to be able to acquiesce in a suspension of disbelief that would have come more naturally to the members of a society nurtured on the reading of the Homeric epics and other heroic legends. Doubtless, Socrates showed an indifference in the face of death consistent with his avowed belief in the benignity of the transition that he was about to undergo, but this was merely the seed from which Platonic husbandry has grown a dramatic portrait of the philosopher as an old man so compelling as to have become an enduring image of the elevation of the mind by reason.

The narration is by the eponymous Phaedo to the obscure Echecrates. A framework dialogue in dramatic form, set in Phlius in the Peloponnese, introduces the main narrative (57a-59c). The choice of the Peloponnese is no doubt partly intended to suggest to the Athenian reader the scandal of Socrates's being more honoured in the sphere of right-thinking Sparta than in his own city. The awe-struck Echecrates is meant to be a kind of leader of the chorus of all future readers.

At the start of the narration proper, the friends of Socrates gather in suitably sombre mood. They do not include Plato but do include two visitors from Thebes, Cebes and Simmias, who play a leading part in the discussion. Notoriously, Xanthippe, Socrates's wife, is sent home with the child for remarking that this is the last occasion on which Socrates will entertain his friends. In her absence, the conversation turns promptly to the merits of suicide. With naïvety traditionally characteristic of his home city in Boeotia, Cebes asks whether a disapproval of suicide can consistently be combined with an admiration for death. Socrates's reply does little to conceal his own apparent longing for death, and, consistently with his stated principle that you cannot tell what something is like until you know what it is, he makes so bold as to claim indeed to know what death is, which he so much esteems. It is the separation of the soul from the body, such that it can go about its business the better for not being constrained by the gross defects of the flesh. Throughout the *Phaedo*, we hear nothing of the division of the soul into three that is such a key feature of the argument of the *Republic*.

Death, then, consummates that process of psychological purification that is the central thread of the philosopher's earthly existence (reflecting a conception of the good life very different from the mere calculation of hedonistic loss and gain which the Socrates of the *Protagoras* proposes as the basis of personal morality). Unlike Hamlet, however, Socrates and his friends are constrained by the thought not of something, but of nothing, after death. Suppose the insubstantial soul evaporates like a puff of smoke on its liberation from the body. What reason have we for supposing that it persists after the death of the body to reap the harvest without which at least one strand in Plato's writing suggests that philosophy and life itself is pointless? This question sets the agenda of the dialogue, which includes three arguments, two objections, a digression, answers to each of the objections, the second amounting to a new positive argument, and a myth.

The first two arguments (63b-77a)

The first argument is based on the idea of the reciprocal generation of opposites. Dead souls cannot be permitted to drop out of being, since they are required, through some unspecified mechanism, as the raw material for new lives. Death, to parody Lucretius, is given never on freehold but always on lease. This curious idea, a kind of law of the conservation of psyche, is found in many idioms and contexts. It is not obvious how seriously it is here being put forward, and it may be partly intended, through its echoes of the Orphic mystery cults, to enhance the impression of the piety of Socrates in a discussion that is in danger of throwing it into doubt.

The second argument (72e ff) recalls the doctrine of reminiscence from the *Meno*. Formal aspects of our cognitive equipment cannot be acquired and so must be innate, but the inaccessibility of many such aspects (those, for instance, connected with our grasp of the theorems of geometry) is most plausibly explained by their instillation into the mind at some remove from its entry into mortal life. This doctrine is now often cited as illustrating the strengths and weaknesses of 'Platonism', its grasp of the central fact that there are structural features of our knowledge of the world that cannot have been acquired by elementary empirical generalisation, on the one hand, and its willingness, on the other, to account for such features, at least in his published writings, in the lurid idiom of mythology rather than the chaste tones of science. The use of the doctrine of reminiscence connects the pre-existence of the soul indissolubly to the validity of the Theory of Forms, as it appears in this dialogue, and so a decision as to the level of irony operating will be determined by the view that we take of the seriousness with which the Theory is being put forward. I will discuss this at the end of the chapter.

As Simmias and Cebes point out, these first two arguments point to the pre-existence rather than to the survival of the soul, although, as Socrates retorts, the argument from reciprocation should bear equally in either direction. In any case, further confirmation is felt to be needed of the immortality of the soul, and, in his third argument, Socrates proceeds by showing the absurdity of supposing the contrary, that the soul is mortal. For something to be capable of being destroyed, we are told, it must be compound, changing and perceptible. All these properties are possessed by the body right enough, but surely not by the soul. Moreover, the nature of the soul, intimately connected with the functions of pure thought and of the domination and control of the body, is close not to the too, too solid flesh of the body but to the immortal gods. It is compatible with this that souls must 'rise in their degree' – we cannot expect the soul of the sensualist to rise so easily to the society of the divine as the soul of the philosopher. Nevertheless, not even the most vicious soul is susceptible of destruction absolutely.

The harmony model

These arguments all presuppose that the soul is a pure substance, characterised by thinking, knowing and willing, but Simmias draws Socrates's attention to another account, the harmony model (85e ff). The soul is related to the body not as a dominant, if transient, occupant but rather as the harmony of a piece of music is related to the lyre on which it is played. The harmony is not, surely, a further thing over and above the lyre; rather, it is best looked on as a kind of higher-level state of the lyre. We do not, philosophers say, need an ontology of harmonies, only an ontology of lyres. Similarly the soul or, as we now say, the mind, may be a higher-level, or as we now say functional, state of the body, and we can dispense with the psychic branch of ontology. It is now widely accepted that some such account of the mind in terms of higher physical states has decisively resolved the metaphysical issue in Plato's disfavour, so that Simmias's harmonic objection foreshadows much in later, especially contemporary, philosophical psychology.

Compared with the profound threat posed by the objection of Simmias, that of Cebes is a pretty footling affair (86c). It amounts to a complaint that Socrates's arguments, while showing that the soul lasts longer than the body, do not show that it is immortal. Perhaps it merely runs through a succession of bodies, as one does jackets, before finally succumbing itself. Life, though no freehold, cannot be rented on a short-dated lease. This objection mistakes Socrates's argument for the immortality of the soul as an argument for its mere longevity, but a bad argument for *A* is not usually a good argument for a minus *X*. In fact, the objection is planted to set up Socrates's final argument, that from causation, which he believes to be conclusive.

Socrates responds by digressing (89a-91c). For many readers, the digressions of Plato are additions which are more important than the work. The present digression is a justly admired celebration of the 'Socratic' preference for the validity of the argument over the comfort of the conclusion. The text of the sermon is that no fate is worse than that of misology, the hatred of reason:

> Let us not, he said, become haters of reason, in the way that
> people become haters of men. For there is no worse thing that
> could happen to anybody than to come to hate rational debate.
> And hatred of reason comes about in the same way as the hatred
> of people. Hatred of people is the product of having trusted
> someone too much and too unguardedly, thinking that he is
> wholly truthful, sound and reliable and then later finding out
> that he is a lying dog, and this on repeated occasions.   (89d)

This is another very familiar rhetorical device, which Plato will use
again in the *Theaetetus*. When the argument reaches a particularly
tortuous or demanding phase, it is useful to break off and celebrate the
edifying purpose in engaging in this sort of discussion. This is a kind of
pep talk which both relieves us of serious thinking for a while and puts
us on our intellectual mettle to return to it after the break.

Braced by the digression, the disputants return to the objections.
Understandably, Socrates's rebuttal of the harmony objection focuses
on the specific rather than the generic features of the harmony model
(91c ff). It is much easier to show that the soul has dissimilarities with
musical harmony than to show that it is in general unreasonable to
suppose that the soul is some kind of higher-level state of the material
body. Socrates also appeals to the apparent tension often observed
between soul and body (as when the soul of Homer's Odysseus steels his
body to endure some scrape), a tension explained in the *Republic* in terms
of the clash of different elements within the soul.

Formal causes and the mind

Part of the refutation of the harmony account is that the soul is a cause,
whereas a harmony is an effect. This idea is now developed at length in
the refutation of the objection of Cebes, which blossoms into an inde-
pendent argument for the immortal soul (96e-109a). The doctrine that
'Mind is the cause' was pioneered by the great fifth-century scientist-
philosopher Anaxagoras of Clazomenae in Ionia, in a formulation,
however, that does not fully meet with Socrates's approval. Mental
causation can only be understood when we have grasped the notion of a
formal cause. A formal cause is, by our lights, a strange sort of cause,
but then we draw the line differently from the Greeks between A's being
the cause of B and B's being explicable by A. Thus, for Socrates in this
dialogue, Beauty is the (formal) cause of beautiful things, Greatness of
great things, Smallness of small things etc. The Forms of the properties

of things cause those properties, and a Form also excludes from itself anything other than its own nature. Thus the Form of Life excludes death, and since the Form of Life in some sense is the soul, this too must be metaphysically incapable of perishing. Strange as we may find the notion of formal causation, it was to influence the philosophies of science and mind throughout the classical period of Greek thought.

The concluding section

The argument from formal causation triumphantly concludes the business of the meeting. There follows a myth, thought by connoisseurs to be one of Plato's more successful (109a ff), describing the soul's passage through the after-life, and then the most famous passage in Plato. The

Fig. 9 The Death of Socrates: The best artistic treatments of the famous scene at the end of the *Phaedo* are inspired by the eloquence and restraint of Plato's description.

description of the death of Socrates is an act of *pietas* by Plato on which it almost seems impertinent to comment. It could be said, however, that part of the reason for its extraordinary success lies in the way that it combines sublime elevation with a certain robust realism. In later rhetorical theory, this would be regarded as a mixture of the high style of elevated passages with the low style of ordinary narrative, and, perhaps partly because of the precedent of the *Phaedo*, such a combination was always highly regarded.

In any case, the ending is a worthy conclusion to the sublime structure of the dialogue. Many critics have regarded it, together with the *Symposium*, as Plato's most perfect composition. It is by no means unique in achieving a harmony between the subject matter of the discussion and its external context, but it does so more strikingly than in any other case. The characterisation of Socrates is more sure and memorable than ever before, and the course of the conversation is beautifully integrated with the evolution of the mood. Both evolve hand in hand, and we form more than ever the impression that life itself is at stake in discussions of this kind. It may well have been the case that Socrates had in fact felt a kind of death-wish, which underlay his conduct in his last hours, but this is transmuted by Plato from mere morbidity to the extraordinary theme of the philosopher's life as a preparation for death.

However, the greatness of the dialogue rests on more than the mere artistry of its construction, the eloquence of its conclusion and the power of its portrait of the hero. What is also striking is that it introduces a metaphysical dimension more extensively and compellingly than any previous dialogue. The doctrine of reminiscence has already been introduced in the *Meno* (81a) and the psychology which goes with it has appeared in various of the earlier dialogues. There have even been anticipations before of the language of the Theory of Forms, but there is no previous dialogue in which so rich a presentation is given of the elusive Theory or in which it is so systematically integrated with other philosophical views.

The 'Theory of Forms'

Use of the Theory of Forms (for short I will refer to it as 'the Theory') is the great characteristic of the four middle-period dialogues, although, as we have said, it is foreshadowed in several of the earlier works and it certainly has echoes in the later ones. It is only, however, in the four central dialogues that it appears to be fully accepted and presupposed in the arguments. It is right to say 'presupposed' rather than 'stated' or 'explained', because at no stage, not even in the extensive discussion of dialectic and the famous metaphors of the *Republic* (507c-516e), is it ever fully set out as a theory. This is evidently paradoxical – the Theory purports to be the official core of Platonism, a benchmark in terms of which other philosophies, such as those of Aristotle, can be measured and yet at no point are we given even a summary statement of it and fundamental uncertainties persist about central features of the key entities, the Forms, that it introduces. Not surprisingly, scholarly debate has raged as to what should be made of this.

The consensus of opinion has tended to favour the view that Plato was himself in some way committed to the Theory. On this assumption, the major questions then become whether Socrates also accepted and perhaps even invented some version of the Theory and whether Plato came to modify or even abandon the Theory in his later career. The enigmatic and elliptic presentation of the Theory still needs to be explained on this assumption, of course, and one promising line that has often been taken is that the dialogues give a more informal and sketchy presentation of a doctrine that was more fully developed and worked out in the internal discussions of the Academy. Although it is now thought unlikely that Socrates himself held anything like the Theory, it remains quite possible that Plato did and that it was indeed more fully stated in internal lectures and discussions in the school, and most contemporary accounts of the Theory offer some such picture.

It is, however, also possible to suggest quite a different explanation. The Theory is not something that Plato, or anybody else, ever actually held (at least not until it was revived by middle and late 'Platonism'). By contrast, references to the Theory are an elaborate rhetorical device. Plato is well aware that the purpose of a philosopher is not to have a theory, much less to reconstruct the social and political world on the basis of it. But he is also well aware that the notion of a study whose purpose is not to generate theories is a strange and possibly at first sight an unappealing one. He is, it must always be remembered, writing for those whom he is seeking to attract into philosophy, and he knows perfectly well that the number of his converts will be much smaller if there is no message for him to sell. There must therefore be a kind of dummy message. He must appear to have a theory to offer. That theory is the Theory, and its elliptical non-statement makes perfect sense in the circumstances. The Theory is also of exactly the sort that would attract newcomers to philosophy. If the Theory is correct, then knowledge of it, gained through philosophy, gives special access to a hidden range of entities, which has a redemptive value for the believer. After long training the philosopher eventually graduates to personal association with the Forms in an ecstatic union which secures his eternal salvation.

This may seem to us to be rather a tall order for any philosophical theory to provide, but it would have had clear resonances in the minds of contemporary readers. They would surely have perceived it as kind of intellectualised version of the appeal made by the mystery cults. We know that it is a striking feature of Greek religion that from around the second half of the fifth century there developed an ever increasing range of cults that offered some version of the model of selective salvation through initiation. Many books have been written on what this phenomenon tells us about Greek religious life and about the decline of the city-state as a political institution and our understanding and knowledge continue to evolve, but it has relatively seldom been pointed out that the supposed Platonic Theory of Forms fits very well into this pattern. Everything about the Theory and about the institutionalising of philosophy that goes with it in the *Republic* is wholly in line with what we know about the mystery cults. In the world of the early fourth century, after the cataclysm of the great war that ended the fifth, there were many people in the Greek world who would nowadays be described as looking for 'alternative lifestyles', who wanted a new structure on which to base their spiritual and intellectual existence. The mystery cults catered for this market (as they were to continue to do up to and beyond the rise of Christianity), and it was also this market, albeit the higher end of it, that Plato was seeking to tap. He was offering philosophy as a way of life and he was well aware that he had to make it attractive in the face of the competing suppliers.

It is, therefore, misguided to think of the central dialogues as providing a rhetorical presentation of the Theory (worked out elsewhere with rigorous precision). Rather the Theory itself is a rhetorical construction to enhance the effect of the dialogues. Indeed, the very contradictions and obscurities of the Theory immediately become natural and appropriate, rather than baffling and irritating, once we realise its essentially religious character. Greek religion allowed the combination and multiple interpretation of objects of worship and thrived on uncertainty, multiple identity and even downright contradiction. This goes as much for the 'official' Olympian pantheon as for the mystery deities and the seemingly endless array of demi-gods, spirits and demons. Some of this flavour is very effectively carried over into the Theory in the dialogues and it greatly enhances their literary effect. Of no dialogue is this more true than of the *Phaedo*, where the Theory first plays a really major role and where the infusion of metaphysics adds especially potently to the profound artistry with which the debate is handled. But the Theory also contributes enormously to the extraordinary literary achievements of the other central dialogues, and we will look next at the remarkable synthesis achieved in the *Republic* before surveying the reflections on his own methods that Plato offers, cryptically, in the *Symposium* and, above all, in the *Phaedrus*.

Chapter 9
The *Republic*

The long period of germination in the works leading up to the *Euthydemus* and the new metaphysical profundity found in the *Phaedo* finally bear fruit in the extraordinary construction which is the *Republic*. The *Republic* is most obviously distinguished by its sheer size (exceeded only by the much later *Laws*), but closer examination soon also reveals a remarkable structural elegance and indeed irony. The framework of the dialogue is that of a debate within a debate, with the central books 5, 6 and 7 being framed by the other seven, and in an admirably subtle manner the conclusion of the central section undermines that of the flanks. There could be no better demonstration of how philosophy evolves through itself.

The central argument

In the early dialogues the view which Plato usually gives Socrates to defend is broadly as follows. Moral behaviour has traditionally been divided into a range of virtues, but this division is ultimately superficial, moral goodness being *au fond* unitary. The possession of such goodness is the greatest possible advantage in life and, indeed, is to be identified with the good life, so badly misconstrued in the advertisements of the sophists who purport to teach it. The key to the possession of goodness is the understanding of the real structure of the world, the prospect of which is held out by philosophy and by philosophy alone. This message, dispersed across the dialogues of the early period, is concentrated into a single remarkable line of argument in the *Republic*, which is dedicated to demonstrating that justice, the cardinal virtue, is more advantageous to its possessor than its opposite, injustice. Put like this, the desired conclusion may seem rather elusive, not to say opaque. What, after all, is it to possess justice? The answer is that, for the purposes of this dialogue, the possession of justice is equated with living a moral life, a life, that is to say, constrained by considerations external to the immediate or even long-term self-interest of the liver. Such a life can be contrasted with one in which the liver recognises no values but the promotion of his own utilities and is in principle prepared to ignore all human regulations and customs and all divine admonitions in the furtherance of this cause. The liver of the latter sort of life may indeed accept the need to abide by the conventions of human society in default of the ability to flaunt them, but he will always regard this as an unsatisfactory position and not tolerate it for a moment longer than it is in his interest to do so.

Of these two lives, arguments for the second, though not unknown, have been produced relatively less often by philosophers, whereas, no doubt, it has always enjoyed the tacit favour at least of all those who reckon that its general application would be in their own interest. Few people, if seriously put into a position of being able to do wrong with complete impunity, the position that Plato dramatises with his famous (or notorious) example of Gyges (359b-360d), would have the natural strength of mind or probity of disposition to refrain from misdemeanour. It is to someone in this position that the *Republic* is ostensibly addressed. He will read it and abstain from crime. The work is the first sustained philosophical defence of the idea that virtue is its own reward.

So described, the project commands a certain respect – who can disapprove of an *advocatus angelorum*? The problem, however, with the *Republic*, and the reason for the withering denunciations to which it has been subjected in the twentieth century, is the way in which it sets about discharging its advocacy. The route to understanding the superiority of virtue over vice lies through the acceptance of a hierarchical structure of the human personality and, thanks to an infamous analogy, an exactly parallel hierarchy in the structure of human society. It is hardly surprising that vilification has been heaped on Plato for all three of the central theses of the *Republic*, the crude functional analysis of personality, the analogy of the mind and the state and, above all, the doctrine of the corporate state whose overall structure and stability is more important than the interests of any of its members.

The first book

It is usually thought that the dialogue as we have it grew out of the work that now constitutes its first book. The decision to extend that work so massively may well have been associated with the plan to add three dialogues to the *Apology*. The first book, sometimes dubbed the *Thrasymachus* by modern scholars, is a characteristic specimen of the dialogues purporting to record encounters with sophists, though the character of Thrasymachus himself is rather more trenchant than most such interlocutors. The discussion, though of uneven quality, bears comparison with that in the *Gorgias*, and the famous introductory setting is as well handled as any in Plato.

Socrates, after a day of pious participation in a religious ceremony in the Peiraeus, the harbour of ancient as of modern Athens, is hi-jacked as he sets out to walk the five or six miles home by a group of young men from a highly respected mercantile family of *metics* (permanently resident non-citizens) and their friends, who insist that he delays his return to the city in order to spend the afternoon in discussion at the house of Cephalus, a senior member of the family.

The respectability and the very age of Cephalus are used both to put Socrates firmly in his 'social context' of being a natural associate of the best elements in Athenian life and to cue the discussion of the rewards of goodness (328b-331d). The serenity with which Cephalus confronts the closing of his life is to be explained by the impeccable restraint that he has shown in the conduct of it. He is an example of that inner harmony and balance that it is to be the message of the *Republic* that one can only achieve through the moral life. Cephalus, however, has reached this position by the light, not of nature, but of reason, and he shrinks from the challenge to engage in an abstract discussion as one might withdraw one's foot from a snake that crosses one's path in the woods. In the contrast between the diffidence of Cephalus and the brash confidence of his son Polemarchus in intellectual discussion we see that gap between the generations that Aristophanes satirises so effectively in the *Clouds*. Cephalus, we are intended to feel, is secure in his untutored knowledge of the good and the true, but his son, being open to discussion, is also open to subversion, and it is this possibility that is the fundamental justification of the work of the true philosopher. This, however, is no mere contingency: the likes of Cephalus have a natural tendency to produce the likes of Polemarchus, and even if this were not so Cephalus himself cannot really be said to be good until he knows that, and why, he is good.

Polemarchus, then, is drawn into the ring and proceeds to receive a routine drubbing at the hands of Socrates (331d-336a). His responses to the invitation to state what it is in which justice consists reveal both his own naïvety and the shallowness of the received morality. Cephalus, the merchant, has already suggested that the redemption of loans is the epitome of justice, and, when Socrates puts the case of the justice of the return of a loan of armour by a man who subsequently loses his wits, Polemarchus moves to what he evidently feels to be the consensus position that the good man helps his friends and harms his enemies, in equal measure and with equal relish. This is a paltry account of the virtue, to be sure, but, even to get it going, Polemarchus must narrow his position down to the view that it is the intention to do good or harm rather than the actual doing that constitutes the morality of the behaviour. His failure to grasp this point gives Socrates the opportunity to invite him to specify some particular way in which the just man characteristically performs his beneficial or deleterious actions, and, when this leads the hapless young man into the usual morass of manifest absurdities, he is able to drive home his deeper point that it cannot ever be part of the intention of the just man to effect that deterioration in another moral agent which is the likely result of the hostility to enemies counselled by the ancestral (at any rate Homeric) morality.

The consternation of Polemarchus, who complies perfectly with the rules of dialectical etiquette, is soon forgotten in the face of the onslaught of Thrasymachus (336 ff). Thrasymachus is the History Man of his time. He is abrasive and uncouth in manner, sullen and graceless in deportment, and his position has that relentless superficiality that sits so well with a desire to shock conventional opinion. Can such a person have existed, or is he conjured from the misty hinterland of Plato's mid-life crisis, soured as it no doubt was by the persisting prevalence of the (to him) facile doctrines of the Athenian left?

The bombshell which Thrasymachus carries under his cloak and which, after some sparring, he is ready to lob is the pithy adage that *justice is the interest of the stronger* (338c). This has the sort of hard-edged cynicism that some thinkers and their acolytes have tended to find attractive. The idea, probably, behind what Thrasymachus is saying is that the conventional broadly co-operative morality that counsels restraint and deference in dealing with others is no more than a tool by which the element dominating any polity will conveniently induce the subservience that they would otherwise have to compel from the rest. The trouble is that Thrasymachus's desire for the compression of the slogan has led him into ambiguity. There are two quite distinct positions that can be mustered beneath the banner of his slogan. On the one hand, he might be saying that it is a moral truth that one should always promote the interest of the stronger element in any association, whether one be that stronger element oneself or not, and that the conventional moralists have merely been wrong in the sort of way in which we now think that astronomers were wrong before Copernicus. On the other, his view could be that morality is an illusion and that the language of morality is merely an instrument for the enhanced control of the weak by the strong. The dominant group in any society merely decrees that whatever suits it is right, and such stipulation must form the basis of any analysis of the meaning of such terms as 'right' and 'just'.

Thrasymachus's uncertainty as to which of these two positions he is so shockingly advancing is exposed by Socrates's challenge that he account for what is to be done by the just man who has received an instruction from some ruler that is patently against the interest of that ruler. On the first interpretation, the just course of action will be to continue to promote the master's real interest, ignoring his own erroneous endeavours to damage it. On the second view the formal and literal edict will be all there is to the moral prescription to which the just man will owe allegiance, and he will do what he is told. Confronted with this dilemma, the initial response of Thrasymachus, prompted by his associate Cleitophon, is to embrace the second option, but he soon thinks that he has found a way of slipping through the horns by denying that the ruler, in the strong sense that he has in mind, can ever be in the position that leads to the dilemma. This, however, merely plays into Socrates's hands by shifting the issue to ground favourable to him, the question of the true nature of the ruler. Whereas Thrasymachus assumes that the unqualified nature of the true ruler will be to exploit his subjects without restraint or respite, Socrates brings him to accept that the true nature of the ruler will be to promote the interest not of himself but of those entrusted to his administration. He does this by a series of arguments based on particularly tendentious analogies with such activities as medicine and being a shepherd which, in common with ruling, involve control over someone or something else. The Thrasymachean model will, by contrast, epitomise governmental folly.

Thrasymachus, resorting to the abuse of the humbug and the prolixity of the charlatan, protests at length that the promotion of the interest of the subject is itself ultimately motivated by the self-interest of the ruler (343b-344e). His interest in their well-being is only conditional on the achievement of his own – the shepherd would not graze if there were no market in sheep, nor the doctor prescribe if there were no fee for his services. The Socratic response to this is that, *qua* shepherd, the shepherd is not interested in the sale of his sheep, only in their flourishing. This being so, being a shepherd is not something that one would do for free, and neither is being a ruler. So, however Thrasymachus is to patch his position, it cannot be by an appeal to the intrinsic nature of the ruler.

This argument is often held up as a paradigm of Plato's use of the Socratic *elenkhos*. Of course, we feel that Thrasymachus has been hard done by, but opinions differ richly on how his chances could be improved, and that, equally obviously, is the point of the exercise. The most popular, and perhaps the most promising, prescriptions for rescuing the cause of Thrasymachus stress the points that morality is a matter of intention not of competence and that the power of the ruler is different from the mere responsibility of the doctor. Plato has indeed been much criticised for failing to allow for the role of the will and the problem of power and its distribution – they seem to form a blind spot in his moral and political vision. However, it is important to see Plato's rhetorical purpose in this much discussed first book. It is in part, as suggested, to whet our appetite by irritating our dialectical instincts, but also to suggest a central idea, i.e., if we reflect on the very nature of a situation in which one party has authority or rule over another, we will come to see it is intrinsic to the arrangement that the former must act in the interest of the latter and anyone who exercises authority in disregard of this will be to that extent irrational.

The remainder of the first book (347e ff) is devoted to the relative advantages of justice and injustice. The Socratic rule – that one can only know what a thing is like in some respect after one has discovered what it is – is not very well observed, and Socrates's three arguments, though sufficient to see off the disgruntled Thrasymachus, are patently, even spectacularly, specious. The weakness of the defence of the wisdom of morality is the cue to the project launched in the second book, to which the rest of the dialogue is ostensibly devoted, that of showing the higher interest of being good. This, however, does not in itself resolve the question of whether the first book was originally written for its role in the whole work or had a previous separate existence which its author subsequently deemed apt for such massive extension.

The official 'solution'

At the start of the second book, Glaucon channels the tacit dissatisfaction with the upshot of the discussion to date into a challenge to Socrates to show, on the assumption that good things or advantages can be divided into three groups, those (e.g. pleasure) desirable intrinsically; those (e.g. vision) desirable intrinsically and for their products; and those (e.g. fitness training) desirable only for their products, to which group the advantages of morality belong (357b-358a). When Socrates allocates justice to that group of good things desirable both for itself and for its products, Glaucon expounds at length and with plausibility that the consensus opinion is rather that it belongs only to the third group, that of things advantageous merely for their results. People are only good, it is widely believed, because otherwise they would either miss advantages or incur penalties or both (358b-361d). The case is most succinctly made by the story of Gyges who discovers a ring which, by making him invisible at will, enables him to commit with impunity whatever crimes he chooses. Adeimantus then corroborates the thrust of his brother Glaucon's point by claiming that the view that morality is only good so long as it is useful is in fact deeply entrenched in the conventional wisdom of Greek literature, education and culture (362e-367e). The challenge that they jointly put is this: why should Gyges bother to be good?

In response to this challenge, Socrates embarks on a description of the evolution and nature of the state, from which it transpires that the Utopia will be a society composed of three strata distinct in nature: a ruling elite of intellectuals, the infamous Platonic Guardians; a supporting caste of those who realise both the advantages of the rule of the best and also their own lack of qualification to participate in it; and the broad mass of people whose merit can consist only in their wholesale submission to the dictates of the philosophers. By thoroughly sophistical arguments, this social structure is claimed to possess all the virtues and conspicuously justice, which consists in the fact that all the organs of this state contribute, by their performance of their proper function, to the harmonious operation of the whole (433b ff).

It seems extraordinary that this model has ever been taken seriously as a contribution to political philosophy and that its author has been construed as so intending it. The details that we are given, in the discussion running from books 2 to 4, of this Ancient Greek Waco, which in any case almost exclusively relate to the education of the Guardian class on which all else is deemed to hang, have, as already mentioned, close affinities with those of a model state satirised in a near contemporary play of Aristophanes. It seems unreasonable to suppose that Plato felt that this would not be recognised by his audience or that his intention was to do anything more than dramatise the absurdity of an encroachment by political science on the territory of philosophy.

If the account of justice in the state is essentially a tease, the account of the personality in the fourth book can be regarded as a parallel attempt to put empirical psychology in its place (435e-445e). Socrates argues that the personality, or soul, has three main components, which, of course, parallel those of the state, being the reasoning, spirited and appetitive faculties. The soundness of this trichotomy is urged in the light of what seem to be empirical, or quasi-empirical, considerations. But, of course, the experimental evidence spectacularly under-determines the sweeping theoretical claim. What are we to make of this? Are we to agree with those solemn interpreters who hold that Plato simply had a rather impoverished conception of the requirements of empirical confirmation in scientific psychology? Or should we embrace the conclusion that the point of this analysis of the personality and its associated account of personal morality is just that it is obviously unsatisfactory?

The stumble into philosophy

The central rhetorical device of the *Republic* is this: that in reading it one should realise that it is impossible to have a real understanding of right and wrong without engaging in philosophy. But, how, if this is so, can we expect Plato to suppose that we can derive any real understanding of moral questions from patently non-philosophical considerations? The contrived failure, even absurdity, of the central line of reasoning in the *Republic* is essential to its message. The defence of morality is impossible without philosophy. To the *Republic,* even more than to the other dialogues, we might apply a celebrated remark which the twentieth-century philosopher Ludwig Wittgenstein made about his *Tractatus Logico-Philosophicus*, that the outer books are like a ladder that one must kick away after one has climbed it.

By the beginning of book 5 (449a), Socrates has produced an argument purporting to show the nature of the good state and of the good person (the argument that we have seen to be a reduction to the absurd of non-philosophical ethics). He is about to proceed to describe the degenerate forms of state and individual and to show the superiority of the good over the bad, when he is interrupted by his audience who demand clarification of some of the details of his ideal state. There are three aspects that call for further explanation, the role of women in peace and war, the place of private property and the family and, crucially, the practical viability of the whole.

The discussion of women, the family and property is justly famous and, indeed, constitutes the real contribution that the dialogue makes to political theory (451b ff). Since the issues of the family and property are not integral to the account of morality, Plato feels free to make serious proposals of permanent importance. The power of the extended family in Greek society remained constant throughout antiquity, conditioning attitudes to both the role of women and the importance of property. Plato is the first philosopher clearly to have seen that private property and the family are crucial ingredients of a pluralistic and liberal society, and his rigorous exclusion of them from the ideal state is a testimony to his understanding of their fundamental incompatibility with rigorous social control. Plato's attitude to women is also remarkable, though it is of a piece with his treatment of the family. His insistence that women can perform the same tasks as men (including that of being a Guardian) has been well-received by modern feminists, often unsympathetic to the rest of his outlook. Plato, however, is a dangerous antecedent for such thinkers, in that he sharpens the dilemma of how it is possible for the lives of women to be liberated and the stability of the family to be protected, while at the same time reminding us of the vital importance of the latter task.

The third aspect that calls for further explanation is how it is possible for Plato's state to exist in reality. It is this issue that cues the introduction of the Theory of Forms. The ideal state, Socrates famously announces (473c), can only come about when either philosophers become rulers or rulers become philosophers; and, of course, this will only be any use, if it is the right sort of philosopher that they become. But what is the right sort of philosopher? The answer is that it is a philosopher who knows the Forms:

> Well, I think that it is necessary, if we are in any way to escape the criticisms you mention, to isolate real philosophers from the rest and explain which is the sort to which we are referring when we make so bold as to say that they should rule. If we make this clear, a defence is possible, since we can show that one group is naturally fitted for philosophy and power while the nature of the others suggests that they should refrain from thinking and follow the leader. (474b-c)

What it means to know the Forms is not, as we know, explained; but it is adumbrated in three stages. First, at the end of book 5, a brief presentation of the Forms is made to those not yet familiar with them (475b-480a). Then, in books 6 and the start of 7, the three famous similes are offered to suggest the metaphysical relationship between our world and that of the Forms. Finally, in the rest of book 7, the further education of the philosopher (beyond the highly censored secondary curriculum set out in books 2 and 3) is presented in its ascending phases, with the details becoming more sketchy as we rise (520e ff). The hints and suggestions given in these central books have been pored over by scholars of all kinds, with the justly famous simile of the Cave rightly taking pride of place. It is impossible to provide any very thorough examination in the space available. All, perhaps, that can be said is that this, the fullest, or at any rate the longest, treatment of the Forms, still leaves it fundamentally unclear whether Plato intends the Forms to be what later philosophers have called realistically construed universals or rather supreme exemplars or paradigms of various admirable qualities. We are reminded yet again that the fundamental point of the introduction of the Forms at the heart of the *Republic* is not to suggest that there is some hidden body of knowledge or argument waiting to be mastered by those with the appropriate training but rather to hint that philosophy is a way of living and thinking that cannot be described but which, when mastered, provides an insight and awareness which both cannot otherwise be obtained and is incommensurably more valuable than anything else on offer in human life.

The rest of the work

At the beginning of book 8 we return to the main argument broken off at the beginning of book 5 and now wholly overshadowed by the remarkable revelations that we have been given since then. Plato has often been criticised for continuing with what may now seem to be an irrelevant line of discussion, and it is certainly plausible that he was influenced to some extent by artistic rather than intellectual considerations, since the discussion of degenerate societies in books 8 and 9 balances the account of the literary education of the Guardians in books 2 and 3. In fact, for all its evident artificiality, the parallel discussion of degenerate states and individuals, freed as it is from the need to contribute to our understanding of the nature of morality, has considerable interest both in its own right and as reflecting on the ideologies of various forms of government and society in Ancient Greece. The final demonstration of the superiority of the good over the wicked life, formally answering the challenge posed at the start of book two, provides a conclusion of suitable rhetorical absurdity to the main line of argument as a whole (529a-b).

The final book, perhaps an afterthought as the first was a precursor, presents Plato's notorious ruminations on the pernicious effects of artistic creativity and his equally notorious Myth of Er. The former has been much discussed, but probably equally much misunderstood. The objection that art, and especially drama, panders to the emotions can be read as much as a demand for chastity in art as for its prohibition. As such, it might well seem more reasonable if we knew more of the evolution of the Greek stage in the fourth century, which was, by what accounts we have, pretty lurid. The metaphysical objection that art cannot reveal us truths about the world is evidently more profound. It can only be said that it has been accepted by some of the best, and rejected by some of the worst, practitioners of all the arts. As for the Myth with which the work ends, it finds few defenders today, and it is not hard to see why this should be so. For a work that has been devoted to showing the intrinsic, or at least internally consequentialist, merits of the moral life, it does seem a kind of surrender to appeal so shamelessly to the pay-off that the just are to receive in another world.

Structural irony

Any summary of the *Republic* must inevitably be selective, and the intention of the above has been to suggest the working of the structural irony that is the most distinctively rhetorical feature of the work. The core irony of structure is that a dialogue which sets out to discover the nature of justice becomes one which offers a parallel account of the structure of soul and state, only to have that in turn undermined by the beautifully crafted suggestion that no answer to the original question can be satisfactory until the inquirer has been fully initiated into the mystery cult of philosophy. The *Republic* thus encapsulates the movement that is in a way implicit in all the other dialogues.

The elaborate ingenuity of the structure is mirrored by the extraordinary diversity of literary effects achieved, which range from deferential courtesy to light banter, to caustic satire, to close analysis, to solemn elevation. The merit of diversification (*poikilia*) is one much stressed in the rhetorical manuals, and it is well exemplified in the *Republic*. At all points, the variation of mood and tone both suits the twist that the discussion has taken and forms a satisfying pattern in itself, which gives a living surface to the complex underlying structure. The work achieves, more fully than any of its predecessors the integration of surface texture and compositional function, never more deftly than when the ironic shift to the core 'digression' is introduced. Moreover, both in terms of its formal structure and in terms of the patterns of surface effects there is a mixture of symmetry and evolution which few other ancient works can match.

All these features make the *Republic* the greatest single achievement of ancient rhetorical theory. It perfectly illustrates both the cut and thrust of altercation and the construction of sustained arguments and narrations. Its use of metaphors and similes is rich but restrained and is certainly in sympathy with what Aristotle has to say about this device. It dovetails characterisation with the drama of the debate in a more telling way even than in the *Euthydemus* and it draws richly on the background of myth and poetry. What must be borne in mind is that all these are specifically rhetorical achievements. Plato had no real model on which to draw in creating the *Republic* and, even after allowance has been made for the element of genius, it seems perverse to suggest that such a construction could have been erected without using the elaborate rules of art that we know to have been available. The *Republic*, by its sheer size and complexity, makes the case for seeing Plato as a rhetorician more clearly and forcefully than any other dialogue.

Chapter 10
The *Symposium* and the *Phaedrus*

The *Republic* is inevitably to be considered Plato's rhetorical master-piece, achieving the complete structural and stylistic mastery for which that discipline strives. It is a consummation of sophistry and oratory, and yet it still denies the latter art. It is remarkable, in a work which covers almost every other possible topic of philosophy, that there is almost no mention of rhetoric as part of the equipment of the philosopher. We sense the attitude is still, at best, that of the disclaimer dialogue the *Gorgias*. The remaining history of Plato's 'middle period' (really, if our argument is correct, the culmination of a continuous process of development) is the story of his movement towards an official reconciliation with the art on which he has so much relied and to which he has made so great a contribution. That reconciliation finally takes place in the *Phaedrus*, but that dialogue could not have been written immediately after the *Republic*, and a vital step towards it was taken in the intervening work the *Symposium*.

The Symposium

The *Symposium* has always attracted a huge amount of attention from scholars, historians and literary theorists as much as from philosophers, as being, alongside the *Phaedrus*, the purest literature in Plato. The work has been subjected to endless interpretation, of widely varying plausibil-ity, and at almost every point it sets off chains of association that rapidly carry the reader far from the text itself. Nothing can be said here about this huge secondary literature of interpretation, except to remark that the *Symposium* has the rare merit of combining the capacity to suggest an almost infinite variety of readings with the ability to be enjoyed and understood more fully in the first instance than any other major work of antiquity.

The social institution on which the dialogue rests operates as follows. In Greek upper-class households men and women lived and ate separately. During the day, the men of the household, free or slaves, would go about their business either in the workshop, the agora or the administrative and military institutions of the city, depending on their station and calling. The women would, for the most part, get weaving. In the evening, no doubt with the occasional night off, the men would congregate at one house or another to while away the hours first, briefly and relatively silently, eating and then partaking, with progressive gusto, in the associated delights of drinking, talk and song. Flute girls would on occasion be introduced to support the last of these activities, though it could no doubt also flourish in their absence. The flavour of the evening could to some extent be moderated by the choice of the mixture of wine and water, ancient wine requiring rather to be debilitated than fortified.

The dinner party which is the subject of the dialogue is held at the house of Agathon, a tragic poet. The guests are: Socrates, brought along by his friend Aristodemus, the distinguished general Pausanias, the doctor Eryximachus, the orator Phaedrus, the comic playwright Aristophanes and, latterly, the young roué Alcibiades, who, at the dramatic date of the dialogue, ca 416 BC, is just embarking on the political career that was to be so disastrous to himself and his city. The dinner follows an evening of celebration for the first victory of Agathon in the tragic competition, so that the decision is taken that the night should be devoted to discussion undistracted by the charms of flute-girls and serious drinking. As an alternative to intoxication, Greek convivial etiquette favoured somewhat formalised displays of friendly rivalry in wit and learning. In this spirit, it is proposed that all the guests in turn should make a speech in praise of love.

The first to speak is Phaedrus (178a f). He stresses the social value of love as a spur to good service to the community and the general search for distinction on the part of the lover and he dilates his remarks into a kind of historical survey of the benign consequences of infatuation, citing the cases of Alcestis, who gave her life for her husband Admetus, Orpheus, who went down to the Underworld to find Eurydice, and above all Achilles. In the *Iliad*, Achilles is warned by his mother, the goddess Thetis, that if he kills Hector to avenge Patroclus then he will himself die soon thereafter. That he was undeterred by this consequence shows, for Phaedrus, the nobility of the character of Achilles (as well as the power of love), for which indeed, in later Greek legend, he was after his death transported by the gods to the Isles of the Blessed.

Pausanias (180c f) follows by stressing, somewhat severely, a contrast to be developed with greater subtlety and felicity by Socrates between the deplorable love of the body and the admirable love of the mind. It is in many ways in the rather crabbed speech of Pausanias that we are most struck by the emphasis, all the more remarkable for being completely unremarked, on homosexual love as the natural, though not the only, topic of discussion. Aristophanes is the next man in, but he cannot come to the wicket because of an attack of hiccups. The doctor Eryximachus (185c f) accepts the invitation both to cure the hiccups and to take his place until the cure has succeeded. The disciplinarian instincts of the military mind are now replaced by the yearning to engage in scientific dissection. The love between human beings is, for Eryximachus, only one form of a general cosmic principle which has a profound controlling role in all the processes of nature. It is evident that Eryximachus is steeped in the writings of the Natural Philosophers, who were prone to use terms drawn from moral, political and legal discussion, such as Justice, Discord, Mind and Love, to characterise general features of the natural world. The generalisation that Eryximachus brings to the discussion also foreshadows the much deeper conception of Socrates but it has a pedantic flavour quite different from the master's ecstatic lyricism.

When Eryximachus has finished, Aristophanes is ready to speak (189a f). His contribution is the first to lift the level of the discussion from the inspired to the sublime. He offers a comic fantasy of truly Attic elegance. There was, we are told, originally a third, hermaphrodite, sex, whose body was equipped with four hands, four feet, two faces and, as Jowett puts it, 'the rest to correspond'. The decision by Zeus to divide this prodigious breed has produced the diversity of passions and attachments that we see around us, the common characteristic of which is that those who feel them are moved by a yearning to be re-united with some whole from which they have been divided off. The speech of Aristophanes is an incomparable *jeu d'esprit*, made all the more remarkable by the fact that Aristophanes is obliquely referred to in the *Apology* as one of those contributing, through his satirical attack in the *Clouds*, to the trial and execution of Socrates.

Agathon (194e f), understandably reluctant to have to follow such perfection, contrives a eulogy of suave counterpoint and urbane harmonies, which is elegant rather than profound, and then Socrates is ready to begin (199c f). The spirit of the *elenkhos* is allowed briefly to cloud the proceedings as he obtains agreement from Agathon that love, rather than being in itself beautiful and good, is the yearning for the beautiful and good. Its excellence is not intrinsic but derived from its object. Against this background, he narrates the account once given to him by the wise woman Diotima of Mantinea. The historicity of this person is usually doubted, and the ironic device of indirect ascription would come wholly naturally to Plato's Socrates in this sort of situation. Her speech, in any case, stresses that love is in the same position as the philosopher, being a mixture of knowledge and ignorance. The key to the understanding of love is to understand not, as with Phaedrus, Pausanias and Eryximachus, the consequences and effects of love, but rather its object. Love, as modern philosophers would put it, is an intentional state. The problem is to specify the intentionality that is its hallmark. For Diotima the content of the desire of love is the immortality conferred by possession of the beautiful. This desire manifests itself across the natural world, but it reaches its height in the desire for immortality that motivates the great statesman and lawgiver. Then, in the ringing conclusion of her speech, she hints that beyond the statesman's love of glory lies the still more abstract love of the philosopher, entranced by that vision of supreme beauty that is afforded by complete absorption in the suprasensible world of the Forms (209e f) and that reaches its peak at the very end of the speech:

> What, then, should we think, she said, if a person were to see Beauty Itself, pure, clear and unmixed, not full of human flesh and colours and all the rest of such mortal rubbish, but were able to see Divine Beauty Itself in its unadulterated form? Do you think, she said, that the life of such a person would be wretched if that were his vision and his activity was worship of, and society with, the Form? (211e-212a)

Thus the Forms, to which access in the *Republic* was taken to be through the arid study of mathematics and logic, can, for the *Symposium*, be approached by the more congenial path of the study and admiration of beauty.

The admirable structure of the dialogue, with three serious speeches, a comic interlude, a display of polished technique and then Socrates's narration of the revelations of Diotima, continues with the famous episode of the arrival of Alcibiades (212c-d). He brings the party back abruptly into the everyday world, but makes his own contribution by describing the extraordinary resistance of Socrates to his attempts at seduction. This broadens out into a general celebration of the personality of Socrates as a philosophical satyr. Further revellers now appear and break up the dinner. The narrator, Aristodemus, dozes off to wake in the morning and find Socrates still engaged in discussion with the two playwrights as to whether the same person can write both comedies and tragedies. Having exhausted them both, he leaves for his usual daily round.

The influence of the *Symposium* on all our thinking about Greece is impossible to overestimate. It has stamped itself on the imagination of

Fig. 10 A Greek Symposium: The institution against which Plato's dialogue is set was well entrenched in the life of the Athenian upper classes and is frequently illustrated on vases such as the one shown above.

generations of readers and has expressed for many the very essence of Hellenism. Its picture of civilised relaxation is irresistible and it has often been taken as the summation of that integration of all areas of life that is plausibly considered the finest achievement of the Greeks. From our point of view, the most interesting thing about the dialogue is the way in which its opens up the possibility of accommodating aesthetic pleasure as part of the experience of philosophy. It is natural, as we have said, to see this as a kind of reaction to the relative austerity and severity of the both the *Phaedo* and the *Republic* (indeed it has sometimes been described as a kind of recantation of the first of those works). It is certainly the sort of dialogue that it would make sense for Plato to write, given his overall objectives, as a sequel to the *Phaedo* and the *Republic*. Both those works give the impression that after the charm of the initial introduction to philosophy which is provided by reading the dialogues themselves, subsequent pursuit of the subject is rather forbidding and restrictive. The *Symposium* suggests that philosophy has as much to do with beauty as with metaphysical reality and that higher insights are not only derived from mathematics. This rehabilitation of beauty then paves the way for the acknowledgement of rhetoric itself as a central part of philosophy, which, in the *Phaedrus*, puts the coping stone on Plato's literary development.

The Phaedrus *and the rhetoric of philosophy*

The purpose of the *Phaedrus* is to pioneer the notion of philosophical rhetoric, which is implicit in the rejection of the rhetoric of Polus and Callicles (but not so obviously Gorgias) in the *Gorgias*, and which is in any case what Plato has been offering his readers all along. But Plato is aware that he cannot construct another dialogue entirely round the subject of the nature of rhetoric. He cannot simply start with the questions What is rhetoric? and How is it related to philosophy? To do so would be to violate the rules of rhetoric, especially the structural irony that is such a conspicuous feature of the *Republic*. So Plato, reverting to the structure with which he experimented in the early dialogue the *Lysis* produces a work of two halves, with the first being devoted to a display of the contrasting types of rhetoric (much as with the ascending series of speeches in the *Symposium*) and the second to an analysis of that contrast. This approach runs the risk of disunity, but in a *tour de force* Plato carries it off through the beauty and nobility of the first section and the intensity and importance of the second.

Only two characters are introduced in the most magically felicitous of all Plato's dialogue settings (227a-230e). Socrates finds the eponymous Phaedrus making his way out of Athens to the country to recover with a stroll from the rigours of concentrating on a recitation that he has just attended by the great orator Lysias. Socrates, intrigued by the speech's brief to persuade a young boy to succumb to a seducer who openly admits his lack of love, agrees to walk with Phaedrus in return for a reading of the speech. After a beautiful description of how they discover a spot on the banks of the Ilissus in which to settle, Phaedrus reads the speech of Lysias. Then Socrates makes a speech of his own, which is a kind of restricted variation on the theme of the first. At this point he makes to leave but is deterred from so doing by his habitual sign, his *daimonion*, which always intervenes to prevent him from committing some moral or religious wrong, in this case insufficient reverence for the god of love, and so stays to deliver a speech in favour of ideal love, which might well be claimed to be the single greatest specimen of ancient oratory to have come down to us. This marvellous speech achieves a new high point of philosophical rhetoric.

It is not quite clear what we are to make of the contrast between the exaggerated enthusiasm shown by Phaedrus for the speech of Lysias that he reads to Socrates and the obvious faults of both its content and its style (230e-237a). It is an exhortation from an older man to a young boy to the effect that it is more in the interest of the boy to succumb to one who does not love him, such as the speaker, than to one who does. It is mean-spirited in outlook, shallow and vapid in argumentation and execrable in stylistic range and variety. We are certainly meant to notice the connection between its moral and formal defects. The poverty of its moral outlook is mirrored in the pedantic monotony of its expression. It appeals throughout to the self-interest of both parties in a most mercenary spirit, and the only point of any merit that it makes is that the lover must be regarded as inherently unreliable by dint of his being acknowledged to be in the grip of a kind of insanity. The speaker himself, by contrast, exhibits to perfection a mentality to which the state of infatuation can only appear as an aberration.

When Socrates in his response hints at the poverty of content of the speech while ironically flattering its style, he lets slip that he could himself make a better speech on the subject, and Phaedrus makes it clear that he will not be allowed to leave without making this good. In fact, however, he is willing only to cover half the ground that Lysias has traversed, the injunction to beware the lover as a man not fully in possession of his senses, and even this much he delivers, as he puts it, with his head covered as a mark of his reluctance.

Socrates's first speech (237b-241d)

The contrast between the speech of Socrates and that of Lysias is evident right from the start. After an elegant invocation to the Muses, he sets his speech in a narrative context by explaining that its speaker is one of many lovers of a young boy who only affects not to love him and who, consonantly with his pretence, seeks to show that the attention of the non-lover is to be preferred to that of the lover. In even sharper contrast with what has gone before is the insistence of Socrates's speaker that the issue can only be resolved after a definition of the nature of love and thus of its effects on those who either are or are not subject to it has been achieved.

The definition of love, which is separated from the rest of the speech by a brief exchange with Phaedrus, is its strongest part (237b-238c). Socrates distinguishes between the innate instinct for pleasure and the rational and acquired instinct for virtue. Love, at least in the presently relevant sense, is one of the excessive and over-developed forms of the former, being specifically the instinct for that pleasure that is derived from beauty. It is indeed a kind of imbalance of the mind and, like the other excessive forms of the pleasure instinct, vaguely discreditable to its possessor. From the definition the speaker passes to the resulting denunciation of the failings of the victim of love with regard to the object of his passion. Conspicuous among them is the fact that the lover will wish to keep his darling in a state of dependency and even subservience, so that he will have no motivation to develop him in body and, especially, in mind. The attentions of the lover of this kind can therefore never be in the long-term interest of the object of his love. (It is a notable assumption of the whole dialogue, reflecting the nature of Greek homosexuality, at least among the upper classes at Athens, that the older man is supposed to play a conspicuous role in the moral and intellectual development of the boy.)

As the speech continues, we have more and more the feeling that Socrates is dissatisfied by what he is saying, even though he is distanced from it by the unnamed *persona* that he has introduced. This dissatisfaction takes a very specific form in the immediate aftermath of the speech, when he receives a manifestation of his famous restraining sign. At various points in his life, Socrates received a kind of premonition to desist from some intended action on the grounds that it would be in some way impious. It is precisely this that he now feels. His denunciation of the effects of love, uncertain as it may have been, is a kind of blasphemy, and he tells Phaedrus that he feels called on to make amends, in the style of the palinode or recantation sung by the lyric poet Stesichorus to appease Helen for suggesting that she was responsible for the Trojan War. This 'palinode' is the great second speech, which is the centre of the entire dialogue and the rhetorical pinnacle of Plato's middle period.

The second speech (243e-257b)

The speech begins with the central claim that whereas love is indeed a form of madness it is not the case that all madness is deleterious in its effects (244b-245a). The states of prophetic and artistic inspiration and of certain kinds of therapeutic possession are all forms of madness, yet patently beneficial. It is notable that Socrates is here more generous, or else more ironic, in his treatment of madness than he is in the *Ion* (535e f). It is, then, so far unclear whether the particular madness of love is beneficial or harmful. This question, however, can only be resolved in the light of a comprehensive survey of human nature. This begins with the demonstration that the soul is immortal since it is the source of its own movement, an idea that was to play a considerable part in the philosophical psychology of the Academy, and moves on to one of the most famous images in ancient literature, the comparison of the soul to a charioteer with two horses in his team. In the case of the human soul, one horse is good and the other bad, since, in the figure, the charioteer is the rational faculty and the horses are the spirited and appetitive instincts which also play their part in the psychology of the *Republic* (439e-443c).

The comparison launches Socrates on the myth that forms the body of his speech. In this extraordinary prose hymn, which has neither earlier nor later peers in the whole body of philosophical literature, he describes how the entire Company of Heaven proceed in an eternal procession of divine chariots around the outer perimeter of the world (252c f). From this exalted state the human soul has a propensity to decline through its innate vice, and it falls to love to restore its wings so that it can again soar to the heavens. Given this redemptive role of love, it is evident that it must be to the advantage of the object of love to respond to the approaches of the one who is possessed by it. The case, then, has already been made, but Socrates further shows the natural tendency of love to inspire this response by suppressing the worse instincts of the soul, symbolised by the bad horse, thus producing the exalted and purified *eros* that we also find celebrated in the *Symposium* (209e). This whole extraordinary performance has obvious affinities with the words that Socrates puts into the mouth of Diotima in that work, but it excels them in the richness of its creative energy, the passionate beauty of its vision and the sublimated chastity of its style and diction.

Rhetoric as philosophy

The contrast between the mean, crabbed and artificial production of Lysias and the magnificent creation of Socrates is so extreme as to make it natural for us to seek for some explanation. In a way this is provided in the remainder of the dialogue, but in a way not. There was an important intellectual industry in Greece devoted to the production of Arts of Rhetoric, manuals on all aspects of the composition, arrangement and presentation of speeches, and even by Plato's time a considerable specialist literature was developing. The *Phaedrus* does to some extent make a contribution comparable to that of the technicians, but the overwhelmingly more important point is just that excellence of speaking cannot be divorced from the more general moral and intellectual outlook of the speaker in the way that the technicians urge. Just as the *Republic* seeks to distinguish true philosophy from its sham, so the *Phaedrus* does the same for rhetoric. And when both activities are fully understood and practised at their best, they turn out to coincide.

The crucial role of understanding and knowledge in oratory is stressed right at the start of the discussion (258d f), and we are clearly meant to see how superficial was the allocation of rhetoric to a mere shadow art made in the *Gorgias*. It is not so much that the *Phaedrus* is a recantation of the *Gorgias*, as should by now be obvious, as that the primary concern of the earlier dialogue is with the misuse of the art, that of the later one with its proper interpretation. The central role given to knowledge makes the present discussion an entirely appropriate place for Plato to launch a new method for the acquisition of knowledge, the method of collection and division (265b ff). This is the ancestor of the method of definition by genus and species and was to have a profound effect on the philosophy of science, logic and metaphysics both in the later Academy and in the Lyceum. It is, indeed, the basis of classical science, notably of Aristotle's system of biological classification, and it is an indication of the achievement of the *Phaedrus* in rehabilitating rhetoric to philosophy that its introduction is not out of place in this context. Beside it the technical devices that Socrates next reviews pale into appropriate insignificance.

The closing sections of the dialogue (277b f) stress once more that philosophical knowledge and especially the insights of philosophical psychology are essential to the rhetorician. The human soul emerges as the proper study of both the philosopher and the orator. The influence of Anaxagoras, the metaphysician, on Pericles, the statesman, is here cited as a paradigm. In a way, this is another formulation of the demand in the *Republic* that the intellectual and administrative elites must ultimately coincide. There follows one of the crucial sections, in which Socrates insists that philosophy is essentially something that cannot be committed to the written word, that it lives only in the discussions and conversations of its practitioners.

The *Phaedrus* is, by any standards, one of Plato's most astonishing achievements. It is a flawless work of art but at the same time offers an inspired and wholly compelling vision of the integration of philosophy and rhetoric into a kind of super-discourse, a sublime illustration of which is provided by the great speech of Socrates. It is hard to praise too highly its combination of inventive power and dialectical control.

With the last section of the *Phaedrus*, Plato's development has reached its natural culmination. In a sense, it is a retrospective justification of everything that he has done up to now. Having shown in practice that rhetoric is indispensable to philosophy, he can now come forward and announce as much. After the achievements of the central dialogues, Plato seems to have felt that he has now made the case for philosophy as eloquently as it can be made and indeed by about 470, a probable date for the composition of the *Phaedrus*, it is likely that the Academy was well launched as an institution in the Greek world (Aristotle came to it as a brilliant student from remote Macedonia sometime in the early 360s). It was in 367 that Plato made his second intervention in Syracuse, which for a while promised to give him the chance to achieve the sophist's dream, political power in someone else's city. He no doubt resumed writing more or less as soon as he returned to the Academy, but, if the scholarly consensus is right to place the *Parmenides* next in his list of writings, it is clearly that he has already begun to adopt the very different attitude to rhetorical philosophy which marks his late phase. There is a clear, and in my view fundamental, distinction between the works before and after this *Phaedrus/Parmenides* divide, the latter, with the spectacular exception of the *Theaetetus*, showing little of the rhetorical panache of the former. The *Phaedrus* is, therefore, the natural conclusion of the story we have been telling of the evolution of Plato as the greatest champion of the intellectual revolution of the fifth century BC.

Chapter 11
Conclusion

We have now reviewed the progress of Plato's rhetorical development up to the composition of the four central dialogues which have traditionally been considered to be the core of his work. The *Republic* has had pride of place as his most remarkable single composition, but I have tried to show how it fits naturally into the overall pattern of his output. The closest that Plato comes to giving a statement of his own conception of the use of rhetoric in the service of philosophy is in the second section of the *Phaedrus*, and I have argued that this should be regarded as applying to all the earlier dialogues. As we have already discussed, there is reason to think that Plato's objectives changed after the composition of the *Phaedrus* and perhaps after an enforced interval in connection with his intervention in Sicily. The later dialogues do not lend themselves so well to analysis in terms of rhetorical technique, although there are still traces of such technique even in the most unliterary of the dialogues, and at least one dialogue, the *Theaetetus,* revives the rhetorical approach of the earlier period.

However, the conclusions of this book apply principally to the dialogues usually thought to have been written before the year 370. I have tried to show that they form a continuous progres᠁ ., though I would not like to suggest that they represent the implementation of a single project conceived in advance. What they do represent is the consistent and constantly evolving application of the rhetorical theory which Plato acquired in his youth to the three objectives of vindicating Socrates, promoting the practice of philosophy and encouraging recruitment to the Academy. It is true that this combination of objectives, no less than the m᠁er in which they were pursued, is unique, but we can clearly see antecedents in the works and the careers of several of the sophists, so far as we can reconstruct them from our meagre evidence.

We know that the practice of writing moral dialogues was widespread among the sophists, and it would have been a wholly characteristic innovation of Plato to take as his hero not a figure from legend but the character of the historical Socrates himself. The general pattern of Socrates's method was, as we have seen, essentially sophistic in origin, and there is nothing in the dialogues to disguise this fact. The portrayal of rival sophists is predominantly hostile, but there are important exceptions to the general critique and in any case the implied disclaimer should not be taken any more at face value than that at the start of the *Apology* (17a-b). It was no doubt a commonplace for sophists to deny that they were sophists, just as it was a commonplace for orators to deny that they were using rhetoric. We find a similar phenomenon among those latter-day sophists who are known as spin-doctors.

If, then, we can conclude that Plato is to be classed with the sophists whom he affects to despise, does this mean that we should revise downward our estimate of him and accuse generations of readers and scholars of having been duped into according him a status as a major original philosopher which is not rightly his? In my view, to do this would be to fall victim ourselves to the art of Plato. It is very largely on his evidence that we convict the sophists of shallow superficiality, and the more we understand about the intellectual development of the ancient Greeks the more we realise what a crucial part was played in it by the sophists and the orators. It is no disgrace, even for so great a thinker as Plato, to be included in this category.

On the other hand, there is a very great advantage to be derived from such an inclusion. The advantage is that we can begin to understand how it was possible for Plato to make such extraordinary progress in the refinement of Greek prose literature, which has played a huge part in the development of all subsequent European prose. If we deny, as it is still standard practice to do, that there is any close connection between sophistic and rhetorical technique and the art of Plato, then we are left with no explanation of how that art was possible. We can only resort to old-fashioned and not very illuminating assumptions about Plato's innate talents. It is no coincidence that the greatest writer of antiquity should have emerged in close connection with the flowering of the sophists. This is something that we should celebrate, not attempt to disguise. For, as the products of an inspired response to the methods of the sophists and orators, the dialogues can be seen as one of the finest fruits of what is rightly called the Greek Enlightenment.

Suggestions for Further Study

1. Describe the social changes that the Greek city-states went through between the Persian Wars and the death of Plato.

2. What common characteristics were shared by the sophists and what influence did they have on Greek public life?

3. How well did traditional Greek education equip pupils to cope with the changing conditions of Greek life?

4. Explain the rise of oratory and rhetoric in the 'open societies' of ancient Greece.

5. How accurately can we reconstruct the career of the historical Socrates?

6. Is it possible to have any real insight into the reasons why an Athenian jury sentenced Socrates to death?

7. Why does Plato never include himself in his early and middle period dialogues?

8. How easy was it for Plato to recruit members of his Academy and what form did the course followed there take?

9. How shocking would a contemporary Athenian have found the model state presented in the *Republic*?

10. Is there an irreconcilable tension between the attitude adopted to rhetoric by the *Gorgias* and that adopted by the *Phaedrus*?

Suggestions for Further Reading

Original sources

Plato. All the dialogues covered have been translated in the following works in the Penguin Classics series:

The Last Days of Socrates, translated by Hugh Tredennick (1956)
The Republic, translated by Desmond Lee (1955)
Gorgias, translated by Walter Hamilton (1953)
The Early Socratic Dialogues, edited by Trevor Saunders (1989)
Phaedrus and Letters VII and VIII, translated by Walter Hamilton (1962)
Protagoras and Meno, translated by W.K.C. Guthrie (1956)
The Symposium, translated by Walter Hamilton (1951)

There is also an excellent translation of the *Republic* by Robin Waterfield in the World Classics series (1992).

Xenophon. The works of Xenophon are less widely available, but the following translations can be recommended:

Conversation of Socrates, edited by Robin Waterfield (Penguin Classics, 1990). Includes Xenophon's *Apology, Memoirs of Socrates* (*Memorabilia*), *Symposium*, and *Oeconomicus*
The Persian Expedition (*Anabasis*), translated by Rex Warner (Penguin Classics, 1949)
A History of My Times (*Hellenica*), translated by Rex Warner (Penguin Classics, 1966)

There is a good collection of the fragments of the Presocratic philosophers in:

Early Greek Philosophy, translated and edited by Jonathan Barnes (Penguin Classics, 1987)

Modern Works

The list of all relevant works would be enormous, but the following are excellent introductory books:

The sophists

Guthrie, W.K.C., *Socrates* (CUP, 1971)
Guthrie, W.K.C., *The Sophists* (CUP, 1971)
Kerferd, G.B., *The Sophistic Movement* (CUP, 1981)

Socrates

Brickhouse, T.C., and Smith, N.D., *Plato's Socrates* (OUP, 1994)
Stone, I.F., *The Trial of Socrates* (London, 1988)

Plato

Annas, J., *An Introduction to Plato's* Republic (OUP, 1981)
Ferrari, G.R., *Listening to the Cicadas: A Study of Plato's* Phaedrus (CUP, 1987)
Grube, G.M., *Plato's Thought*, University Paperbacks (Methuen, 1935)
Hare, R.M., *Plato* (OUP, 1983)
Melling, D.J., *Understanding Plato* (OUP, 1987)
Murdoch, I., *The Fire and the Sun: Why Plato Banished the Artists* (OUP, 1977)
Pappas, Nickolas, *Plato and the* Republic (Routledge, 1996)
Rutherford, R.B., *The Art of Plato* (Duckworth, 1995)

Rhetoric

Cole, T., *The Origins of Rhetoric in Ancient Greece* (Baltimore, 1991)
Kennedy, G., *The Art of Persuasion in Greece* (Princeton, 1963)
Vickers, B., *In Defence of Rhetoric* (OUP, 1988)